MAXIM GORKY

ROMANTIC REALIST AND
CONSERVATIVE REVOLUTIONARY

I. Maxim Gorky as a young man. From a photograph.

MAXIM GORKY

ROMANTIC REALIST
AND
CONSERVATIVE
REVOLUTIONARY

✣

RICHARD HARE

LONDON
OXFORD UNIVERSITY PRESS
NEW YORK   TORONTO
1962

Oxford University Press, Amen House, London E.C.4

GLASGOW NEW YORK TORONTO MELBOURNE WELLINGTON
BOMBAY CALCUTTA MADRAS KARACHI LAHORE DACCA
CAPE TOWN SALISBURY NAIROBI IBADAN ACCRA
KUALA LUMPUR HONG KONG

PG-3465
H3

*Printed in Great Britain
by Richard Clay and Company, Ltd.,
Bungay*

CONTENTS

171925

ILLUSTRATIONS

FOREWORD

No substantial or up-to-date study of Maxim Gorky's life and work has appeared in English since Alexander Kaun's *Maxim Gorky and his Russia* (1932). Many of the various English translations of his novels and stories are out of print. But the vast majority of Gorky's scattered and voluminous writings have been systematically assembled for the first time in the thirty-volume edition of his collected works, published in Moscow by the Soviet State Publishing House (1949–55). Certain works of his, originally published in Berlin, have been omitted from this edition, and I have commented on the suppression in my book. Some revealing private letters, held in America, were first published in *Harvard Slavic Studies* (Harvard, 1954) and in *Letters of Gorky and L. Andreyev* (New York, 1958).

It has been asserted that some manuscripts and diaries, written by Gorky, were seized by the secret police immediately after his death and destroyed, by Stalin's orders. There is not enough evidence to put this beyond doubt, and we still do not know for certain whether Gorky died a violent or a natural death.

I have had the opportunity to hear illuminating personal accounts of Gorky's later years from people who knew him well. For obvious reasons, my informants preferred to remain anonymous. Nor can they be held responsible for any judgements which I have expressed. I also owe a debt of gratitude to some generous-minded scholars, especially to Ernest Simmons, Robert Tucker and the late Michael Karpovich, and to Miss Dorothy Galton for valuable help with the proofs.

R. H.

I
LEGEND COMPETES WITH FACT

MORE than any other outstanding Russian author, Maxim Gorky (1868–1936) became a victim of the unstable intellectual fashions and social movements with which his personality and literary work have been entangled. After a short period of sensational international renown, which reached its peak in the first decade of the present century, he began to subside into the ambiguous position of an eccentric literary classic and a controversial political figure.

During the early years of the Soviet regime he again emerged into the limelight as a courageous critic and discriminating humanitarian, and in the nineteen-twenties, during his residence in Germany and Italy, he became a symbolic bone of contention between the vacillating friends and enemies of the newly established Bolsheviks. Finally, after his return to Russia in 1928, the *émigrés* bitterly condemned him as a renegade to their cause, while the organs of Soviet publicity started to build up a monumental political legend, linking his name with the triumphal march of international Revolution. His appeal soon spread to thoughtful, social-minded literates of India, China, and Japan, where it still prevails, while it has simultaneously declined throughout the Western world.

Meanwhile a whole contemporary attitude to Gorky has been entirely shaped by Soviet educational policy. His current Soviet reputation is mainly based on his much advertised function as an intellectual stepping-stone between the two eras of Russian life separated by the October Revolution. While he has probably received his due as the last giant of nineteenth-century Russian letters, he has been disproportionately idolized as 'the mighty proletarian writer', the original pathfinder of an emergent Soviet culture, and misleadingly described as a personality belonging to a theoretically prescribed structure of the future, rather than to a living historical past and unpredictably fluctuating present.

In this exemplary and legendary capacity Gorky has for many Soviet Russians long since blotted out the greyer image of the grimly economic Marx. And there has rapidly accumulated a vast unwieldy mass of letters, sketches, reminiscences, bibliographical and police records, and a spate of articles voicing conventional praise of Gorky, published in a never-ending stream ever since the nineteen-twenties.[1] A recent grand symposium, reviewing the principal achievements of Soviet literature up to date, published by the Academy of Sciences, devoted six out of ten contributions entirely to aspects of Gorky.[2] Its frontispiece (and sole illustration) depicts a genial avuncular-looking Stalin and an emaciated, aged Gorky, smiling at each other as they stand together in the Red Square in Moscow. Thus on all sides he has been covered with such a mass of fulsome and repetitive advertisement, that the ordinary Soviet mortal must now penetrate a dense adulatory barrage, if he ever wants to see the real Gorky face to face.

As a rule Soviet revaluations of nineteenth-century Russian figures take their cue from some remark extracted from the holy writ of Lenin, whenever Lenin deigned to mention them. But in this case Lenin's politically guarded judgement of Gorky is strikingly remote from later Soviet canonization of him. Lenin may have kept a soft spot in his heart for Gorky, but much as he admired his talent, he was continually chiding him for his political vagaries and temperamental unreliability. He violently denounced the school which Gorky founded in Capri (1909) for training a selected group of Russian artisan leaders; he went so far as to outlaw all participants in it from the Bolshevik Party, and finally attained his object by terrorizing the school into extinction.

He complained that Gorky in his *Confession* (1908) 'befogged

---

[1] The best of these are articles and studies by V. Desnitsky, S. Balukhatuy, and N. Piksanov.

[2] *Voprosy Sovyetskoi Literatury*, Moscow–Leningrad, 1953.

the material origin of all ideas'. In one characteristically abusive letter he accused Gorky of giving constant help to his *bête noire*, the new *democratic priest*. 'A Christian priest deflowering little girls (I have just read of one in a German newspaper) is far less dangerous than a priest without a cassock, a democratic priest overflowing with plausible ideas—because it is easy to expose, condemn and chase out the former priest, but not nearly so easy to chase out the latter. And you, knowing as you do the frailty and pitiful instability of the Russian philistine mind—why Russian, is the Italian any better?—you tempt this mind with the sweetest poison. . . . Your whole attitude to God is through and through reactionary.'[1]

That word 'reactionary' (even more than its fashionable antithesis, the word 'revolutionary') has become so painfully hackneyed and soiled in the service of political mud-slingers, that it has quite lost its wider original meaning. Its narrow political usage failed to distinguish between stale convention and live tradition, and it assumed a queer belief in absolute historical change, like the eruption of a gorgeous butterfly out of a dull chrysalis grub. It deliberately confused the man who clings passively to the dead hand of sterile formulae, with the active conservative, who struggles to save the inherited treasures of prolonged human effort and skill from being trampled underfoot by degenerate or callous contemporary philistines. Throughout his life Gorky showed himself to be a whole-hearted *reactionary* in the latter nonpolitical sense, and the fact that Lenin plainly told him so is significant. For Lenin, however shrewdly he valued Gorky as an advertising agent, and as a weapon to promote the Communist Party's rise to power, remained distrustfully aware that Gorky's talent, free from ideological tutelage and dictation, might inflict mortal wounds on the sacred body of Party orthodoxy.

For Gorky constantly defended the surviving culture of the past, and fought to save it from the latest onslaught both of bourgeois and of Bolshevik vandals. Unfortunately such vigorous conservative instincts, aroused whenever human values stood in

[1] Alexander Kaun, *Maxim Gorky and his Russia*, p. 440, London, 1932.

danger of destruction by bestial or bogus substitutes, his hatred of banal mediocrity, tepid tolerance of the intolerable, and what he described as 'my organic disgust for all politics'—these features remain, either distorted, or carefully tucked away, in the background of his legendary Soviet picture. Moreover, this official Soviet *iconography* has unduly handicapped the reputation of Gorky in the West, where interest in him steadily and understandably declined, almost inversely to his build-up by the Stalinist regime. Nor has the Soviet attitude to Gorky changed perceptibly since Stalin's death. He remains firmly planted on the same official pedestal, untouched by any public controversy. Only through having been so heavily and categorically labelled by his Bolshevik compatriots as their exclusive laureate, has he turned elsewhere into one of those dated semi-classics, artificially discussed in literary circles, but rarely read, and still more rarely understood for his own less spectacular but honest merits.

It can hardly be disputed that Gorky's rugged, strained, and patchy talent fell far below the artistic genius of his immediate predecessors, Tolstoy, Turgenev, or Dostoyevsky. But he compensated for his spasmodic crudity and uncouth lack of mental discipline by the refreshing novelty of his themes, the exactitude and range of his observation, and sometimes by the frank aspiration of his strong, ebullient, many-sided personality. For he always tried to reach beyond the sphere of humdrum current literature, to grasp the startling educational powers of literary art in moulding peoples' minds (whether for good or evil), and he remains a key to the formidable Soviet attitude towards the state's responsibility for training human feelings by means of 'culture' under state control. But from start to finish Gorky could never reconcile his natural honesty and clearsightedness with the perfectionist sermons in which he also gloried. He could never blend the naked chaotic life around him, which he saw transparently, with the turgid lyrical exhortations and consoling falsehoods, in which his chronic social conscience compelled him to indulge.

He admitted his own double-faced attitude quite plainly when he gave a double answer to his Soviet questioners in 1928 (*How I learned to Write*). 'To the question, why I began to write, I answer thus—from the pressure upon me of an exhausting poverty-stricken life, and also because I had accumulated such a load of impressions that I could not stop myself from writing. The first reason impelled me to try to instil into that poor life such fanciful inventions as *The Song of the Falcon and the Grass-Snake, The Stormy Petrel,* and *The Legend of the Burning Heart.* Thanks to the second reason I began to write stories of a more "realistic" character, such as *Twenty-Six Men and a Girl* and *The Orlov Couple.*'

That excitable tendentiousness, which might have impeded Gorky's popularity and success elsewhere, considerably promoted it in Russia. For his urgent social message—and Russian literary critics then, as now, were concerned with little else—gave something palatable to every section of the reading public—to sentimental admirers of the under-dog, militant social reformers, and even blasé Philistines, craving for poignant new sensations.

Furthermore, his bold and buoyant mood sharply distinguished him from older authors like Korolenko, who had treated with a more serene restraint the same desperate world of doomed wanderers and motley misfits. The fresh frank eloquence and defiant indignation of this self-taught wonder-child from the underworld flashed like a streak of lightning over the quiet twilight horizon of the Russian eighteen-nineties. He satisfied the craving of the mentally blunted and apathetic reader for sharper shocks from life in the raw. He hypnotized despondent intellectuals by his philosophic *bravura.* And he roused the hopes of discontented artisans by appearing to be the champion of the same rebellious outcasts whom he vividly described.

Russian critics and publicists, when led astray by their incurable *penchant* for abstract catchwords and for the mental drama of logical polarities, have often handicapped the fewer but more genuinely creative Russian artists. In Gorky the same conflict became a civil war. For he combined acute power of observation with cruder critical gifts, so that the spontaneous writer in him constantly wrestled with his *alter ego,* the aspiring but half-baked social philosopher and would-be public benefactor. The clear-sighted Tolstoy pointed to this rift in Gorky when he told him: 'It is strange that, with every right to be bitter and malicious, you remain kind. You are very bookish: that is bad. I don't understand your entangled brain, but your heart is sensible.' (M. Gorky, *Recollections*, 1923.)

Gorky knew of course, even better than Tolstoy, the length and breadth of Russia, and he remembered only too distinctly everything he had endured and seen there. His overloaded imagination was all the more haunted by nightmares of painfully sickening experience, and these provoked him to take refuge in beautiful illusions which consoled and soothed. Though his world extends far wider than the sphere of any previous Russian author, it inevitably lacks shape, measure, and harmony, and so do nearly all his writings. He never tried to follow Goethe's maxim: '*In der Beschränkung zeigt sich der Meister*'. ('A master reveals himself by setting his own limits.')

A journalist of genius in the way he reported revealing incidents, lit up the essential and discarded minor details, he constantly overreached himself in trying to draw cut and dried conclusions from events he had observed. Such conclusions were not called for by the facts, but they were forced upon him by the harsh and unrelenting pressure of organized radical opinion, which always preferred pedantic social schoolmasters to genial artists, and drove many gifted Russian writers into false untenable positions, exasperating to their own conscience. Later, in trying to blend inchoate contemporary upheavals with the charm of ancient legend, he distorted both into a dully regimented literary school.

But his positive and lasting achievements lay elsewhere, and he ended, rather unexpectedly, by making the nineteenth-century Russian classics (with the notable exception of Dostoyevsky) more widely read and loved in his own country than the work of any later Soviet authors. His own books have been printed in larger numbers than those of any other Russian writer, and selected ones loom large in Soviet educational establishments and on public library shelves. Yet most Soviet readers still seem to prefer Tolstoy or Chekhov—as he did himself. To try to sum up this paradoxical protean man, by labelling him the first great *proletarian writer*, merely provides another dusty cliché which obscures his real qualities, and exaggerates his obvious defects. It does no justice to the honest and unforgettable pictures which he gave of the human Russian environment before and even after 1917.

II

CHILDHOOD AND YOUTH

In social origin Gorky (Aleksei Peshkov) was not, strictly speaking, *proletarian* at all, for he was neither artisan nor peasant. Born into the provincial Russian middle class, he revolted vehemently and permanently against it. He himself describes his father, Maxim Peshkov, as a *meshchanin*, member of the lower middle class. His maternal grandfather, Kashirin, who brought him up, had started life as a Volga barge hauler, but rose to be the respected chief of the dyers' guild in Nijni Novgorod. His grandfather on his father's side, Savatiy Peshkov, had been a common soldier, was promoted under Nicholas I to officers' rank, but later exiled to Siberia as a punishment for brutal treatment of his subordinates. He used to amuse himself by hunting his son through the forest like a wild animal, pursued by yelping dogs. Friendly neighbours managed to remove the boy from his paternal tormentor, and he was trained to be an efficient carpenter and upholsterer. In 1868 he married Kashirin's daughter, despite the furious opposition of her ambitious self-made father, who had planned to raise her higher in the social scale. He still rose to a respectable position, for in 1871 he became manager of the steamship harbour in Astrakhan. But within a year he died of cholera.

His widow and four-year-old son, Aleksei, then returned to Nijni Novgorod. Towed slowly in a barge along the Volga from Astrakhan to Nijni, the little Aleksei started to absorb the atmosphere and setting of his many future stories. His amazing memory later recalled how from the broad centre of the majestic river the towns and villages, appearing on its banks, looked in the distance like miniature toys, made of gingerbread. The child of four remembered every detail of this voyage distinctly, and how he was moved to tears by its strange beauty and excitement. In the same year his grandfather Kashirin sold his big two-storied house in Nijni with its side-wing and garden. The old couple moved into a modest bungalow, which also had to house the reduced dyer's shop.

Throughout Russia, during this period, the skilled small-scale craftsmen were being relentlessly driven out of business by new factories, capturing the market through cheaper and quicker methods of production. The personal mood of the Kashirin family fell into line with the deterioration of their special trade and social status, in the name of economic progress. It accumulated the oppressive tension of mutual hostility, distrust, and embittered irritation. Gorky's uncles, Mikhail and Yakhov, soon separated from their parents, but continued to quarrel vindictively about their right to appropriate their old father's savings. In one of these wild family brawls Mikhail broke his mother's hand with a stick. He soon degenerated into an incurable drunkard, liable to break out into hysterical fits of violence. He could not face the bitter truth that he, the son of a once prosperous town elder, brought up in the lap of luxury and plenty, was now compelled to work in grinding poverty and squalor, saddled with an ugly wife, who grumbled at him day and night.

Amid the daily torments of this peculiar family hell, Gorky found consolation in his delightful grandmother. This almost un-believable and saintly woman opened his eyes on a fascinating inner world of imaginative power. Though she crossed herself ritually in front of ikons, and observed the orthodox religious festivals, her real God was pagan and mysterious. No human beings could see him without being struck blind, but she said that she had seen angels when her heart was pure. She felt happy that, out of the eighteen children she had borne, fifteen had died in infancy. She thought that God had taken mercy on them and made them into angels. When she danced in the lamplight to the gypsy servant's gay guitar, her heavy body grew as agile and graceful as a cat's, and a warm smile lit up her plain old face.

B

Though completely illiterate, she knew by heart an inexhaustible number of folk-tales, legends, and ancient popular songs. She used to tell them quietly, in a sing-song voice, bending over the spellbound child, fixing on him her eyes with their dilated pupils 'as if she were pouring into my heart some energy which uplifted me. . . . Before she came into my life I seemed to be fast asleep, hidden in darkness, but as soon as she appeared, she woke me, drew me out into the world, surrounded me with an intricate network, wove it into multicoloured lace, and became my lifelong friend, the nearest to my heart, the dearest and most understandable person. Her innocent love of life enriched me, and filled me with strength to endure the hardships which awaited me.' (*Childhood*, 1913.) The innate feeling for vigorous rhythmic prose conveyed through oral folk-tales, the magic of a legendary past, the stoic courage to persevere in a disgusting present, all these were firmly instilled into Gorky by his grandmother. He in no way exaggerated the immense spiritual debt which he owed to her. Without her care and guardianship in childhood he might never have grown into a powerful writer, or even into a civilized and responsible human being.

Gorky's mother, on the other hand, an insipid and commonplace woman, seems to have meant nothing positive to him, although he dutifully tried to love her. She lived in terror of her domineering father, and Gorky bitterly resented her second marriage to his worthless stepfather. We know this from his early introspective sketch, *Analysis of facts and thoughts whose interaction dried up the best parts of my heart* (written in 1893). He had mixed feelings for his grandfather, who taught him to read the scriptures, and beat him savagely at intervals. Gorky could not help admiring the old man's dare-devilry and felt fascinated by his spurts of verbal wisdom. But he hated his wild rages and bestial treatment of his grandmother.

School provided no alleviation or escape from home. He felt hurt and humiliated to find that his grandmother's fairy tales failed to impress his obtuse schoolfellows. When they all showed off to him about a book they knew called *Robinson Crusoe*, but which he

II. House of Gorky's grandparents in Nijni Novgorod, now renamed Gorky, where he lived in childhood.

had never read, he determined to buy it for himself. For that purpose he stole a rouble note which he found lying about at home. It turned out to be enough to buy both *Robinson Crusoe* and Hans Andersen's *Fairy Tales* (which he infinitely preferred) and also some white bread and sausages which he shared with the boys.

One day he found his stepfather kicking his mother as she lay prostrate on the floor, and attacked him in a fury with a table-knife. After this unsuccessful attempt at murder, he was hustled back in disgrace to his grandparents' home. The old man had gone almost crazy from avarice and irritability. He shamelessly begged money from all and sundry, complaining that his family had conspired to ruin him. To earn a few extra pennies Gorky became a rag and bone merchant while still at school, and together with a friendly gang of vagabond boys he rummaged in rubbish heaps or stole planks and poles from the Volga barges. Soon afterwards his mother died. His grandfather told him gruffly one morning: 'You are not a medal hanging round my neck,' and turned him out into the street to fend for himself, without either money or friends, and with hardly more than a scrap of elementary school education. It happened, thus, that Gorky, though born into a prosperous middle-class milieu, became at the age of eleven a homeless wanderer, an outcast from all settled society, which he understandably began to despise and hate.

In Russia the impersonal blows of large-scale capital development destroyed the craftsman and the guild before even the latter had grown established or mature. Gorky and his family were among the innumerable victims of this rapid and relentless upheaval. But a still more disturbing feature of Russian capitalism in the eighteen-seventies was that it failed to provide any firm expanding system to replace the more static order which it overthrew, or to re-absorb the many people whom it had displaced. The newly-founded banks and industrial concerns showed no stability and inspired scanty confidence. The number of bankruptcies multiplied with bewildering speed, and in their wake followed an ominous spread of mass unemployment.

Many peasants freed from serfdom in 1861 had migrated to the nearest towns. Others, unable to pay their redemption dues, were sinking into rural paupers. During the prolonged industrial depression of the eighteen-seventies and eighties, factory managers were reluctantly obliged to get rid of numerous redundant workmen. Unemployed artisans wandered aimlessly from place to place, while hungry peasants abandoned their villages in the vain hope of finding food and work elsewhere. Thus hordes of able-bodied vagabonds began to infest the length and breadth of Russia. In the early eighteen-eighties their number was estimated to have reached the alarming figure of five million.

Although the Government introduced a number of sensible humanitarian factory laws during this period, it made no attempt to solve the fundamental economic crisis by resorting to bolder, far-reaching remedies. On the contrary, despite its boundless autocratic powers, the Government's direct intervention proved to be pitifully feeble, hypocritical, and half-hearted. In 1881 a group of state officials, including the notorious Procurator of the Holy Synod, Pobyedonostsev, the Minister for Internal Affairs, Count Ignatiev, and a couple of Metropolitans, circulated to local authorities the code drawn up to regulate a new organization called 'The Society for the Improvement of Public Work'. The code went little further than pious observations of this kind. 'The bitter experience of other countries has convincingly demonstrated that the lack of protection, poverty, and ignorance of the masses make them readily receptive to every kind of Utopian doctrine. . . . Therefore it is essential to teach them now the right kind of productive labour . . . and simultaneously to encourage their moral and religious development on the basis of reasonable and honest work.' [1]

The futility of this Government propaganda resided in the plain fact that it did nothing whatsoever to practise what it preached, and to provide either 'reasonable' or 'honest' work for millions of idle vagabonds. Neither did it force them to do productive work of any kind. The picking of hemp and sticking together of paper bags gave some temporary employment through

[1] I. Gruzdev, *Gorky i yevo vremya*, p. 62, Leningrad, 1938.

local charitable organizations, but these were pathetic improvised palliatives, designed, as the *Nijni Novgorod Trade Paper* (1881, No. 236) sententiously declared, 'to give the poor workman a chance of justifying himself before God, not to live idly on charity, but to earn bread by the sweat of his brow, as the spiritual and civil laws demand'. Such absurd inefficiency in handling a national economic crisis did far more than cruelty, or administrative severity, to undermine relics of public confidence in the autocratic government.

Thus Gorky joined the horde of vagabonds, not as their born or natural equal, but as an angry outsider, whose fortunes had fallen from a higher level than theirs had ever been. He regarded himself as worthy of far better things than the exhausting physical hardships and insecurity of a casual labourer's routine. 'I started active life as a housepainter's apprentice,' he wrote, 'then I baked rolls, painted ikons, fed horses, dug the ground for various purposes, including graves for corpses, became in turn stevedore, night-watchman, gardener, tried many professions, and everywhere felt more or less out of place. I reached such a stage of toughness that I began to count unemployment more tiring than work, acquired "nerves", pains in the chest, and some experience of life.' Though Gorky was impelled by destitution rather than by a mere desire to rove, he knew how to make a virtue of necessity, and could later say: 'My tramping throughout Russia, though not provoked by any wish to be a vagabond, yet served my need to find out where I was living, what kind of people surrounded me.'

It is high time for us to recognize that the ordinary tramp made little personal appeal to Gorky. As he frankly admitted later: 'Most of the people in whose society I wandered neither rose to great heights nor sank to profound depths, but were as colourless as dust and wearisomely insignificant.' Indeed, their monotonous similarity oppressed his mind. 'Most people are five-copeck pieces, current small change—the only difference between them is the year in which they were coined. One is worn, another nearly obliterated, but they are all of the same value, made of the same

material—and all sickeningly alike.' (*The Passer-by*, 1919.) Gorky
has often, but rather unjustly, been accused of glorifying tramps
as picturesque protests against a sombre sanity. More often he observed them truthfully, whether they were drab or colourful, but
for the drably average tramp he felt hardly more than abstract
sympathy, sometimes bordering on contempt. And even if he was
ready to admire and like simple, kind-hearted and industrious
people, he seldom seemed to meet them. Nor did he show much
sympathy for prosperous or self-satisfied artisans. He preferred
outcast specimens, but those who made his heart beat faster are
striking, strange, and quite extraordinary characters.

He later found a strong emotional link between the better
narodnik intellectual and the down-and-out vagabonds with whom
he mixed, and in both of them echoes of his own deep-rooted feeling of apartness from organized society. 'It was enough for me to
go out on the street and sit for an hour by the gates, to recognize
that all those cabmen, porters, labourers, officials and merchants
did not live as I do. . . . The people whom I respected and believed in were strangely alone, alien, even superfluous to that
majority, who in their dirty and cunning ant-like labour meticu-
lously built up the heap of life, which seemed to me thoroughly
stupid and murderously dull.' (*My Universities*, 1923.)

Weariness of the mass of ugliness and cruelty which he everywhere encountered, a craving for enough will-power to conquer
that weariness, a vague vision of created beauty as the only lasting
consolation, if not the true goal of life (but as yet crudely divorced
from it)—those were the entangled but related motives which
gave integrity to Gorky's early literary work. It seemed to him
that the yearning to find some compensating moral beauty (especially in its total absence from the real environment) alone im-
parted a sustaining sense to otherwise grossly degraded human
beings. That is the underlying theme of one of his finest stories,
Twenty-six Men and a Girl (1899). That girl appeals to the abandoned workmen, not as a physical woman, but as a Goddess of
Mercy, a vision from a purer world apart—until the cynical soldier wins his bet and manages to seduce her. But that gives the

signal for the workmen to break loose, to curse their fallen idol, and themselves sink to the level of vindictive savages.

Gorky grew unhappily aware that divergent strains at work within him, in particular the rebellious outcast and the aspiring knight-errant, pulled him in opposite directions. 'One person, knowing too much that was loathsome and filthy, suspicious of people, burdened with disgust, dreamed of a quiet and lonely life, of travelling to Persia, retiring to a monastery, of becoming a forester or a night-watchman—the further away from people the better. The other person, baptized by the holy spirit of honest and wise books, observing the triumphant power of the common-place and horrible, feeling how easily that power might wring his neck or crush his heart with its dirty boot, strenuously armed himself to be ready for every fight, and like the hero of a French romantic novel, drew his sword from the scabbard.' (*Among People*, 1918.)

For the young Gorky at this time Persia presented an oriental symbol of escape through foreign travel. He had watched with fascination the Persian merchants at Nijni Novgorod, sitting im-mobile in the markets, smoking their long *narghil* pipes. Their liquid, dark, nostalgic eyes looked omniscient to him. Among the ikon-painters to whom he was apprenticed in Nijni, he had noticed a similar craving to escape from everyday routine into fantastic make-believe. A few of these craftsmen approached their work with reverence, convinced that they must impart to their painted madonnas, Christs and saints, some inward spiritual power to strengthen and console their future beholders. But for most of them the business of ordinary life, including their work, remained as irksome as it was for him. Apart from the final paint-ing of the face and hands, the processes followed in these image-workshops had grown too minutely specialized, mechanical, and unrelated to each other. They therefore gave scanty and diminish-ing opportunities to satisfy strong creative instincts. The versa-tile master, Zikharev, could paint sacred faces equally well in the Byzantine, the 'Frankish', or the Italian manner. All the expensive copies of the famous *miracle-working* ikons of Smolensk and

Kazan used to pass through his hands. Though he took pride in his skill, 'These prototypes have bound us;' he used to complain. He sought relief elsewhere, and habitually joined his comrades in boisterous but joyless orgies. Gorky found his companions agreeable fellows. But the drab monotony and filthy conditions of the workshop soon palled on him, and, as he caustically observed, he was by nature ill-equipped to practise patience, 'that virtue of cattle, wood and stone'.

At the age of fifteen he moved on to the town of Kazan where, encouraged by a student friend, he decided to improve his mind by study at the local university. Arriving with one rouble in his pocket, he lodged in the cellar of an abandoned house, which smelt of garbage and dead cats. 'That basement proved to be one of my most instructive universities,' he wrote afterwards. He began to study for an examination to obtain the diploma of a village teacher, but found it hard to squeeze the 'living, difficult and temperamentally flexible Russian language' into the 'narrow petrified forms' of grammar, and on learning that he was too young to qualify, he gladly abandoned this last attempt at acquiring a badge of conventional education.

He recognized that his hopes of social advancement through systematic study had proved to be in vain, but he wasted no regrets on that fiasco, and soon found fresh comfort in the company of dock-labourers and thieves. Among them he reverted to his more natural element and began to feel revived 'like a piece of iron plunged in burning coals'. But an old receiver of stolen goods with the acute instincts of his tribe, told Gorky that he would never feel at home among the tricks of thieves, or manage to transform himself into a hardened criminal. 'You have another path to follow,' he observed, 'for you are a spiritual man.' On being asked what he meant by this oracular remark, the old man answered unexpectedly: 'You are moved by curiosity, but you have no self-interest.' Gorky himself explained his moral scruples differently. He attributed his salvation from sinking into a hunted life of crime to the fact that imaginative books had awoken in him obscure but energetic aspirations, which forced him to aim higher than the gross behaviour which prevailed around him.

For the first time in Kazan, he came into contact with young intellectuals who belonged to conspiratorial political organizations, and secretly studied in cellars the *forbidden* works of Chernyshevsky and John Stuart Mill. But economic doctrines and quantitative analysis, set out with all their intricate theoretical formulae, seemed deadly dull and plainly superfluous to Gorky. He found more congenial company in a circle of poor students who resolutely earned their living at the same time as they pursued their studies, and used to meet at the shop of a grocer called Derenkov, whose humdrum business concealed an exciting library of 'illegal' books. While some of these youths impressed him by their pure altruistic outlook, he found many of them over-excited by pretentious newspaper articles and long abstract words. Their intense complicated arguments seemed to him naïve, and pitifully irrelevant to the needs of the hard labouring life which he knew too well.

He was also upset to learn from local prostitutes that their 'educated' clients, especially theological students and government clerks, showed themselves far more perverse and vicious in their physical demands than did the common people of the town. For their part the students considered him a rough diamond, and he felt some resentment in being patronized by inexperienced youngsters, who were inclined to treat him with alarmed but cautious suspicion, as race-conscious white men eye a well-dressed negro. 'A negro wearing a silk hat' was the nickname attached to him later by the hostile and sophisticated Merezhkovsky circle in St. Petersburg, who also mockingly referred to his romantic tramp hero as 'Smerdyakov with a guitar'.

Spurred on by dire necessity, Gorky next took an arduous job as apprentice in an underground bakery. Working there fourteen hours a day, he could spare neither time nor energy to see more of his student acquaintances. He found himself 'cast into a black hole where men writhe like earth-worms, and then seek forgetfulness in vodka-shops and the cold embraces of prostitutes.'

The moment they received their wages, his fellow-bakers tried to forget their long hours of drudgery by spending every penny they had earned on their habitual relaxation. The young apprentice often accompanied them, but he explained: 'I did not drink, and I had nothing to do with women. For me books still took the place of these other forms of intoxication.' Good books cleansed his soul, he said; they gave him a clear and calm conviction that he was no longer alone in the world and would not go under.

Meanwhile the fastidious chastity of this vigorous and awkward youth annoyed or embarrassed his comrades, and made ordinary women mock at him, for he longed to meet women more like the fascinating heroines in his favourite French novels. A painful inward conflict preyed upon his mind. At the age of nineteen he felt more emotionally at sea than ever and, despite many spasmodic efforts, he had signally failed to find even a tolerable mode of settling down to live, either with manual labourers or vagabonds, still less with the educated professional class. His failure to rise above routine wage-slavery, except in day-dreams, his anger against himself and his cruel nomadic fate, drove him to despair.

In December 1887 he bought a cheap old revolver and attempted to commit suicide. He succeeded only in puncturing one lung, but was fated to suffer from the after-effects for his whole life. In a note found on him when he was picked up and taken to the hospital, he had written the following sardonic lines: 'I beg to render responsible for my death the German poet Heine, who first invented *toothache of the heart.* . . . I ask that my body shall be dissected and examined in order to find out what sort of a devil lived in me for these last months.'

After his recovery he departed to the village of Krasnovidovo to work for a Ukrainian shopkeeper called Mikhail Romas, who helped him to regain his self-respect, and did far more than Kazan University to widen his education. One of those hardly credible idealists thrown up by the emotional ferment of nineteenth-century Russia, this man devoted his life to working for the degraded peasants' welfare, although he knew that most of them either hated or distrusted him. He vainly tried to win their confidence by selling them merchandise at a lower price than any other shopkeepers. He had served a term of exile in Siberia, and refused to take the oath of allegiance to Alexander III in 1881.

He taught Gorky never to be deceived either by sentimental talk about the peasants, or by amiable advances from them. Though often helpful and kind individually, 'good beasts', the moment they gathered together in an excited crowd he knew that they could behave more vilely than a pack of wolves. Coarse and dissolute, with a wolfish look, sly and treacherous 'slaves of the soil', they made village life gloomy and unreliable. One villager, called Kukushkin, a born peasant who had bettered himself, remarked with unflattering frankness about his fellow-peasants: 'We made a mistake in defeating the Tartars; they were worth far more than us.'

Gorky's best friend in the village, a gay and charming fisherman called Izot, was found one day drowned in his capsized boat, his skull battered to pieces by blows from an axe. Romas remarked without bitterness that the mob 'always hates honest men, always destroys its prophets and saints. But do not condemn prematurely. Everything will change for the better, slowly, but at least enduringly.' Soon afterwards the same peasants tried to blow up Romas by stuffing his firewood with gunpowder. Finally they succeeded in burning his little store and dwelling-house to the ground.

Romas lost all his possessions, but his local enemies slyly insinuated that he had set his own place on fire. The climax came when a sullen but cowardly mob started to throw bricks at him and Gorky from a safe distance. Both escaped without injury, but Romas had to leave the district. Object lessons of this kind left an indelible mark on Gorky. He compared his latest encounter with real peasants to the Kazan students' favourite talk about pitying and loving the *common people*. Remembering how the students had read and declaimed Nekrasov's woeful poems with tears in their eyes, he felt sure that he could no longer be sustained on that cloying diet of bitter-sweet poetic sentiments.

The hackneyed and endlessly discussed ideals of abstract humanism, that warmed-up eighteenth-century European dish on which Russian intellectuals had been feeding for so long, began to sicken him. To its latest local incarnation, the belief that the Russian common people had become the sole surviving embodiment on earth of wisdom, spiritual beauty, and kind-heartedness, Gorky gave the curt reply, 'I never knew such people.' Nor did he ever deceitfully ascribe such virtues to his tramps. Many years later, recuperating in Berlin after the first exhausting years of the new regime, he looked back again on the old *narodnik* sentimentalists. 'Where is that good-natured thoughtful Russian peasant, tirelessly searching for truth and justice, about whom nineteenth-century Russian literature told the world so convincingly and in such noble language? In my youth I painstakingly searched the villages of Russia for such a man and failed to find him. I found instead a grim and cunning realist who, when he could gain by it, knew how to play the part of a simpleton. He invented many tales and proverbs, the incarnation of his hard life's experience. He said, among other things: "Don't be afraid of devils, but be afraid of human beings." ' [1]

It is hardly true to say of Gorky that the moment he got rid of one illusion he hurried to embrace another. Unlike many disappointed ex-*narodniks*, who later became grim Marxian converts, he rarely tried, except perhaps in his novel *Mother*, to adorn urban artisans with the halo of emergent glamour which had departed from the fading peasant image. His wanderings brought him into touch with too many real disturbing characters, who challenged with equal force both inherited attitudes and new-fangled efforts to believe. The people he had met never encouraged him to set up new idols to worship in the twilight of the old. In any case the Russian artisan was an ex-peasant, rooted in the village, so why should he be better than the peasant? Gorky soberly recorded his perplexing spiritual adventures and encounters, and pondered

[1] *O Russkom krestyanstve*, p. 24, Berlin, 1923.

over their far-reaching, puzzling import, without, as yet, jumping to practical conclusions.

A teacher of history, the son of a priest, had told him: 'We invented the idea of progress in order to console ourselves. For without slavery there can be no progress, without the subordination of the majority to the will of a minority, mankind will come to a standstill. In trying to make life so much freer and easier for everybody, we have merely made it more complicated. We raise more and more machine-workers, whereas only the peasant, the producer of food, is really needed.'

The Kazan police officer, Nikiforich, had impressed him by the way he explained the mysterious control and magnetism which the Russian state exerted over all its subjects. 'An invisible thread, like a spider's web, goes from the heart of His Imperial Majesty Alexander III through all his ministers, His Excellency the Governor and subordinate ranks, down to myself and the lowest soldier in the army.' The revolutionaries had gone wrong, he said, because they failed to understand that such sustaining power remained indispensable. Inferior Poles and Jews, or Russians in the pay of the Queen of England, tried to break that *invisible thread*, while they cleverly pretended, of course, that they were acting for the benefit of the people.

After he left Krasnovidovo, Gorky started to wander from one village to another with his friend Barinov. Taking odd jobs on barges and in the harbours, they slowly worked their way down the Volga to the Caspian Sea. For a time they joined an *artel* of Tartar fishermen near the mouth of the Volga. Then Gorky moved inland to Dobrinka, where he found employment at the railway station as a night-watchman. He had to protect the warehouses from roaming Cossacks who stole whatever they could find, not on account of dire poverty, but to get extra money to buy drink. They regularly bartered stolen sacks of flour for vodka. The station-master himself, a scoundrel with a huge black beard, was said to have beaten his wife to death. It turned out that he also stole regularly from the freight wagons and spent the proceeds on orgiastic parties, which he mockingly nicknamed *The*

Monastic Life. Gorky described this harrowing experience in his autobiography and in his story *The Night Watchman*, and added the self-justifying comment: 'I penetrated everywhere, without sparing myself, and thus learned many things which for me personally might have been better left unknown, but which are necessary to tell to other people.'

The station-master used to invite local notabilities, the assistant district chief of police, the owner of the town's soap factory, and a one-eyed pock-marked deacon, who brought his own guitar. Together with selected women guests they ate and drank abundantly. The young Gorky would then entertain them by singing the most heart-rending folk-songs from his repertoire. Soon they all began to sing and dance with abandon. Gradually they inflamed one another and worked themselves up to tears, embraces, and frantic outcries. Finally they undressed all the women, started to examine them and praise their bodies, and then 'there began something indescribable, nightmarish'. Gorky stayed and observed these orgies until the very end, although he said that they aroused in him disgust and pain, mingled with pity for the women, tortured by men who were roused to frenzy in what resembled a religious ceremony of savages. Yet he recorded that when he described these happenings later to some of his civilized urban friends, he felt in them a scarcely hidden envy for such wild diversions.

The first young woman to play an important part in Gorky's life embroiled him still further in his mental entanglement and frustration. In 1891 he met Olga Kaminskaya, an alluring, widely travelled and accomplished lady of Bohemian habits, who was then married to a vague talkative revolutionary called Boleslav Korsak. Gorky declared his love for her and found it was requited. But thereupon the lady coolly explained that she could not possibly leave poor Boleslav, because he was so weak and unprotected, whereas he, Aleksei, brimming over with the lusty strength of youth, could manage very well without her. This artificial *impasse* infuriated Gorky; it brought to boiling point his latent hatred for weak and ineffective characters.

In the abrupt rejection of his healthy feeling it dawned on him that a vast amount of energy was wasted on dimly negative people, who deserved little sympathy, and least of all benefited by the abundant encouragement which their betters so unprofitably bestowed on them. And he began to formulate one of his dominant ideas, that stupidly misdirected, sentimental, and indiscriminate charity lay at the root of many major Russian ills. By pampering the unskilled poor, it led to chronic idleness and irresponsibility, and it failed to pick out worthier, prouder individuals from the less deserving, who always clamoured for help. By showering benefits on unworthy people, it made them a burden to the more talented, vital, and enterprising. He admitted that he *felt a certain truth* in the words of the Kazan police officer, Nikiforich. 'Pity demands an enormous amount of expenditure on poor-houses, prisons, lunatic asylums, on unnecessary and even pernicious people. We ought rather to help healthy people, to save them from wasting their strength in vain—whereas we go out of our way to help the sickly. On account of this confusion the strong are weakened, while weak people sit on their necks.'

When criminals, impostors, idlers, and every specimen of moral and physical deformity, turn into objects of sentimental solicitude and morbid public interest, they tend to multiply in numbers. Gradually these parasitic creatures undermine and ruin a society which prefers to pander to them rather than to stamp them out. The early recognition of this tendency around him led Gorky to fight strenuously against a meek or mawkishly humanitarian attitude to life. That explains why he condemned so vehemently Dostoyevsky's strained idealization of suffering for its own sake, and detested his delight in abjectly submissive characters, although that did not save his own work from being visibly infected by Dostoyevsky's pathological traits.

Unfortunately Gorky drew no clear distinction between making the best of inevitable hardships and surrendering to the brute force of circumstances. For him meekness could never be a modest fortitude, but exclusively a vice, a nimble adjustability to vile powers, a treacherous elasticity of soul. He had heard too often the gnat-like whimpering of many Russians, who not only en-joyed bowing their heads under the lash of needless evils, without uttering a single word of protest, but even went out of their way to invite harder blows and crueller suffering. He said that such people made him feel like a hobbled horse straining to break loose from a swarm of gadflys. And he despised the 'little fellow', who kissed the boot which kicked him and wants to be loved for his blatant inferiority.

III

THE LURE OF THE VAGABOND

GORKY'S standpoint when he began to write his stories bears a striking affinity to Nietzsche, whom he had read in the early eighteen-nineties. His friend N. Vasiliev had translated *Thus Spake Zarathustra* into Russian in 1889. Indeed some of Gorky's illiterate tramps talk oddly as if they had learned to echo purple passages from Nietzsche. Yet one should not exaggerate the influence of single books and outside sources, when Gorky's own mind, with its mass of sharp half-digested impressions, was moving independently in the same direction. For these apparent points of contact were also widespread signs of the times elsewhere.

From three separate geographical extremities of Europe, three nearly contemporary imaginative writers had arisen, Gorky, d'Annunzio, and Rudyard Kipling. Allowing for the unique flavour of traditional national cultures, all three had certain novel qualities in common, in addition to a curious link with Nietzsche: a taste for exotic scenes, for strong-willed *amoral* men, impetuous and unreflective, yet proud and self-reliant, masters of their own fate, sometimes born leaders of lesser men. But whereas d'Annunzio's heroes are bathed in a rather remote historical glamour, and Kipling's often bear the devalued hallmark of a single master race born to rule inferior breeds, Gorky's vagabonds remain more personally picturesque and earthy, and show less idealistic falsification or patriotic prejudice.

His able-bodied tramps, gay or angry, who drink, fight, steal, and spit on the whole world, resemble neither Rousseau's noble savage, nor Auerbach's stolidly virtuous country yokel, nor Nekrasov's mute and martyred serf. They may incorporate the

c

last desperate spasm of the artificial eighteenth-century yearning to return to an idyllic mother-nature, but they are neither innocent, honest, nor industrious. Moreover Gorky admires them frankly, not for underlying or potential virtues, but for their openly destructive vices. 'I liked their anger with life, their mocking hostility to everything and everybody, and their carefree attitude to themselves.'[1] So long as he is young, vigorous, and healthy, he can afford the luxury of being a law unto himself. The tragedy (for him) begins when this vital misfit exhausts his energy in revolt, beating his hard head against the harder stone wall of a hostile or unresponsive human society. He weakens in the unequal struggle, and as he grows older, either dies of discouragement, meekly submits, or sinks into the helpless apathy of an *ex-man*.

Gorky had often watched this degradation taking place, and was afflicted by its cruel pathos. Though in the end it provided soiled and shoddy raw material for turning men into social revolutionaries, it provided him with ample food for thought. 'He was a more terrifying phenomenon than I was able to express,' Gorky admitted, 'terrifying above all in his boundless despair, his reckless contempt for himself and life.' The jolly daredevil is soon beaten down into the ragged and decrepit inmate of a doss-house. He sinks into a damp and dirty cellar, reeking of stale fat and kerosene, fit for nothing except to lounge about, talk endless philosophy, and curse his fate. He can no longer even drown his sorrows in a generous ocean of vodka. A wearisome spent figure, his charm rapidly evaporates. And the reader, overcome by tedium, wants to lay down the flagging story which began so buoyantly and boldly.

If some of Gorky's tramps now appear to us fantastic, improbable figures, we should remember that he drew them straight from a fantastic real life. He never invented them. After he left Krasnovidovo in 1888, he wandered far afield, through the Don Basin, the Ukraine, and Bessarabia, as far as the south coast of the Crimea. His personal encounters there emerged later in some of his finest documentary stories and reconstructed fairy-tales,

[1] I. Gruzdev, *Gorky i yevo vremya*, p. 70, Leningrad, 1938.

Chelkash, Malva, The Old Woman Izergil, and *My Travelling Companion.* In July 1891 in the village of Kandybovka (Kherson Province) he saw a naked woman, streaming with blood, dragging a cart along the main street, while a bearded ruffian, her husband, lashed her with a knout from the driver's seat, and a ribald crowd of villagers applauded him. The knight-errant in Gorky got the better of him, and he tried to intervene to release the woman, but the peasants nearly beat him to death for his unavailing pains. Their local custom still countenanced such a punishment for an adulterous woman, little more than half a century ago.

To a limited degree Gorky's picture of vagabond types rounds off a native literary tradition. He completes the long portrait-gallery of honest Russian Hamlets, pathetic Don Quixotes, and so-called superfluous men, sometimes 'our best men', as he recorded in his *Childhood.* The disgruntled outcast proletarian is thrust upon the Russian scene as the final mental outcome of bored, frustrated, or resentful aristocrats, like *Evgeny Onegin* and *Pechorin,* and ineffective though poetic middle-class intellectual misfits, like Turgenev's *Rudin.* But there the legitimate comparison must end. For the last-comer is infinitely more destructive, more ominous than any of his elegant and cultivated predecessors. He emerges, unlike them, stripped of the last emotional and occupational roots. He has become the naked symptom of a raging social epidemic, for which plain economic mismanagement and human weakness may be held responsible. For him, personal moral queries and poignant soul-searching have lost all relevance. Has he become 'superfluous' because he is too good for humdrum human society, or because he is too bad for it? Have *they* rejected him, or has *he* rejected them? Is he truly braver and more resourceful than the average settled citizen (as he likes to think) or is he a depraved and boastful lazybones? What right has he to revile the settled town-worker and the industrious peasant, and regard himself as the neglected salt of the earth?

No exact answer can be found, because the monstrous wave of human discontent, petty envy and self-assertion swept balanced moral reasoning aside. Indeed the spreading swarm of hungry tramps threatened the whole structure of Russian society. They might be as varied in temperament as they were in origin— the gypsy with his blood-feuds, the gentle wandering monk, the *holy idiot* cunningly exploiting Christian charity, the *déclassé* professional man, the unemployed student turned bitter Nihilist, and —predominant in numbers—the uprooted peasant and the workless artisan. But all alike began to glory in their anti-social acts, the same fierce surge of anti-social indignation fused them together in their fate. 'Though each was filled with disgust for the other, they all nourished a helpless hatred against the whole world.' (*People that once were Men*, 1897.) The issue cried out for a clear and workable decision. Either the uninhibited resentful tramp would undermine the whole society and drag it down with him, or society must take drastic action to eliminate the tramp by finding a new constructive place for him within its ranks.

It is to Gorky's credit that he recognized the tramp as a more ominous and deep-seated phenomenon than any transient and local victim of economic maladjustment. He also brilliantly distinguished that *internal* temperamental urge to vagrancy (deepseated in many Russians and nomad Asiatics) from the involuntary vagabondage imposed by unstable employment and the threat of hunger. His best stories illustrate this clear-sightedness. His first published one, *Makar Chudra* (1892), shows the primeval tramp *by temperament* in the figure of the roving gypsy. That elemental religion, which united the voluntary tramp with the real gypsy, is simply the worship of boundless but unrealizable freedom. The gypsy pays a heavy price for it in undergoing danger and grim tests of endurance; he earns and wins his own hard personal freedom. He never takes it for granted, and its savour is quickened by his rejection of any compromise with outsiders. All that gives a touch of wild and haunting beauty to the atmosphere of *Makar Chudra*.

The diabolical gypsy girl Radda, and the gifted young Loiko Zabar, both sacrificed their love for one another to a passion for personal independence, verging on insanity. The girl, determined to humiliate the proud young man, knocked him over with a whip, and demanded that he should bow down to her in front of the assembled tribe. Loiko recognized that he must either tame her, or forfeit the independence which he valued more than life. But what man can tame a tiger? He plunged a knife into the heart of his beloved in order to save himself from slavery to her. Her father then performed the ritual of family vengeance, and killed Loiko with the same knife. Only their necessary death imparts a grandeur to their boundless, absurd pride, rescues it from futility, and vindicates one of Gorky's much-abused maxims: 'The madness of the brave, that is the wisdom of life.'

Gorky's next major story, *Chelkash* (1895), develops with more subtlety and force the new theme of justifying the voluntary vagabond. Chelkash, though honestly described as an inveterate drunkard and a skilful thief, none the less towers above the simple peasant lad, Gavrilo, whose modest ambition is to earn enough money to buy a plot of land and then return to till his native soil. Korolenko (like Tolstoy) found fault with Gorky's strained and indignant heroes, whom he nicknamed *cerebral romantics*, exhibitionists, disgustingly in love with their own personalities. But he considered *Chelkash*, though near the border-line, a successful work of art, because Gorky had proved able to let the main character speak and act in gusts of absolute sincerity, without manipulating his inner flow of thought and feeling.

Indeed, despite the author's obvious prejudice in favour of Chelkash, it is the latter's strong unpredictable emotions and flashes of honest doubt, which make this character so intimately alive. Chelkash lures Gavrilo into crime by glowing accounts of the reward he will receive—a triumphant re-entry to his native village, a home of his own, a bride, the prospect of becoming 'king of his own realm'. But while he cunningly enlarges on the joys of peasant prosperity, he gets carried away by an unexpected longing for his own peasant childhood, by memories of the gentle breeze wafted through his native air, bearing the affectionate voice of his rosy-cheeked mother and the firm sensible remarks of his giant father. In that moment of involuntary recollection, it suddenly dawned on him what he had in fact become, a thwarted and lonely outcast. Self-pity, vain regret, and envy for the peasant lad invade and agitate his mind.

But a little later, another violent change of mood sweeps over him as he watches Gavrilo in the toils of greed. Maddened by the sight of so much money, losing all sense of shame and measure, Gavrilo falls on his knees before Chelkash and begs: 'For Christ's sake, give me that money, what good is it to you? You will squander it in one night, while I will need it for years. I will pray for your soul in three churches, for your salvation. . . . You will throw it all away . . . but I will invest it in the land. . . . You are as good as lost already, while I . . . give it to me.' Boiling with indignation and contempt, Chelkash hurls the whole packet of rouble notes at him. Watching Gavrilo's radiant face, distorted with the ugliness of greed, and uttering sharp cries of lustful joy as he squirms in the sand, Chelkash feels a glow of pride that he, a vagabond thief, torn from all ties of home and kindred, could never cut such an abject, mean, and despicable figure. The silly lad, losing the last atom of self-control, then blurts out that he had thought of knocking Chelkash on the head with an oar, and running off with all the money. For nobody would miss a man like him or make a fuss about his disappearance.

Chelkash, roused to a new pitch of fury, snatches the money back from Gavrilo and walks away. After a few paces, he falls unconscious to the ground, stunned by a stone which Gavrilo has thrown at him. Once more the mood alters abruptly. Gavrilo embraces his ex-employer's feet and begs for his forgiveness. Chelkash, recovering consciousness, spits straight into his eyes. 'Forgive me, for Christ's sake,' moans the contrite peasant lad. 'You don't even know how to commit a crime,' Chelkash retorts contemptuously, and pushes the pile of banknotes in his face. 'Nobody will find out what you have done, but you have earned a reward. Here it is.' Thus the two men parted, but the rain and sea soon obliterated the bloodstains and other imprints of their little drama. Chelkash had satisfied his brigand's code of vanity by sacrificing his ill-gotten gains; Gavrilo had gained his money, but lost his peace of mind.

The story, *Affair with the Clasps* (1895), provides a more matter-of-fact account of an ordinary simpleton, a tramp by habit rather than by inclination, an *average* type to whom Gorky rarely pays any marked attention. Mishka is a good-natured drunkard, undertaking any job which will earn him enough kopecks to buy a glass of vodka, but never sticking to any single kind of work long enough to acquire professional skill in it. Such men as he and Semka could dig trenches and clean up garbage heaps, but when they tried to build a hen-house it proved to be beyond their architectural ability. In this story they quietly walked off with the nails and planks provided for the job by their employer.

Their sense of hostility to the outside world is chronic, but muffled by a numb and passive melancholy, by 'a preoccupation with earning money, and very feeble reactions to anything outside that concern'. In their free time, which was always more than they wanted, they day-dreamed. Semka steals the silver clasps from the Bible of an old woman whose well they had cleaned out. Mishka feels conscience-stricken and buys the clasps back from his companion for one rouble. He then returns and hands them back to the old woman with a few simple words of explanation: 'You say we are all beasts and dogs; by God, that's true enough, it seems to me! . . . And then I thought, perhaps this book is the old lady's only comfort. In any case, will people pay much money for the clasps? Hardly. . . . But together with the book they stand for something.' The old woman prides herself on having made a convert, asks him solemnly if he had understood the words she had read aloud from the Bible. 'How could I understand? Have people like us ears for God's word?' But she insists on reading the whole passage aloud to him again. The wretched Mishka, racked with hunger and boredom, listens to her sermon until he can endure no more. If only she could have shown the common sense to let him go at once. But no, she must talk and 'drag the veins out of my body'.

Closely akin to Mishka is Konovalov, in the story of that name, another kindly giant who wanders with a puzzled smile through the world which handled him so roughly. But such

good-natured and straightforward simpletons are not prom-
inent in Gorky's sketches from the lower depths, and they are
even more notably absent from his later pictures of the merchant
class.

The *Orlov Married Couple* (1897) breaks fresh ground. It depicts the ugly victory of the vagabond temperament over the
golden opportunities which it throws away so recklessly. Orlov is
his own worst enemy. Society cannot honestly be blamed for his
decline and fall. He digs his own grave with open eyes. One of
Gorky's most firmly constructed stories, it brings to life a profound conflict between two contrasting Russian types, and is
rarely marred by his clumsy philosophic ramblings or tiresome
moral exhortation. It also reveals how narrow was the dividing line
between the discontented provincial artisan and the incipient tramp.

A restless but quite efficient cobbler lives and works in a dismal
cellar. He gets drunk regularly and beats his wife. The knowledge
that he is wholly in the wrong only makes him hate her all the
more, for his black emotions are much stronger than his will and
reason. Thus their barren days drag on like the links of an endless
chain, binding together in futile mutual irritation two people who
at one time had loved each other. From time to time Orlov's
guilty conscience pricks him, but only enough to make him tell
his wife that he beats her out of melancholy and not for his own
pleasure. He laments to her that he was born with a demon of
unrest in his soul. His wife explains that she can bear no children
because he has kicked her too often in the stomach. He begins to
wonder why he ever married. 'I would be better off as a vagabond, hungry but free. . . .'

One day a sanitary inspector enters their damp and filthy cellar
dwelling. An epidemic of cholera is spreading through the district.
It has to be stopped. He instructs them how to clean and disinfect
their place. His practical zeal and healthy energy arouse in the
Orlov couple an influx of strange new feelings. Grigory is amazed
but worried when he observes how clean, orderly, and luxurious
is the new hospital for cholera victims. Appetizing food and
plenty of it, even bottles of wine, and truly maternal treatment.

Yet he himself lived in a rotten hole 'where even the devil doesn't bother to spit at you', while people writhing in the spasms of death received abundance showered on their unworthy heads. Surely it would be better if all this money could be spent year by year in helping healthy people to live less dismally.

Tempted by a good salary and a welcome change of scene, he decides to go with his wife to work in the hospital. He starts to feel that others value his ability, yet the change still leaves him inwardly dissatisfied. He pined for a wider outlet to release the mighty strength he felt within him; he longed to perform astounding feats which would command applause from thousands. He visualized a proud inscription on his grave: 'Here lies Grigory Orlov who saved Russia from the scourge of cholera.' At the same time he was angry with himself that he could share none of the doctor's pity for their patients. He felt too strongly how wasteful it was to cure sick people, when the life to which they returned was worse than any cholera convulsions. He soberly believed that, if the Government wished to kill off the surplus population of Russia, it could do so most economically by forcing them to migrate and work themselves to death in an uninhabited, wild territory.

Grigory's cravings and misgivings disturbed his wife. She wanted a more even-tempered and affectionate husband, not a moody megalomaniac hero. Occasionally when his renewed kindness reassured her, she began to feel that they had at last been lifted out of their dark hole, and settled down in a more spacious world. But these were fleeting moments, seldom repeated. Matryona felt none of her husband's need to think and judge beyond the immediate present. Her keen intelligent work was valued in the hospital. People were kind to her, and as she responded, so she grew in moral stature. For the first time she saw by contrast how bestially they had lived before. And she knew that a return to that old state of numb wretchedness would be intolerable. Moreover, she could now defy her husband when he became drunk and violent, and hold her own against him. In his turn Grigory started to fear her, to recognize that she had grown too strong for him.

In a last defiant fit of rage he beat his wife again, hurled insults at the doctor, and then left the hospital forever.

He did not want to grasp his opportunities. He preferred to throw them away, ruin himself, and thereby demonstrate his invincible love for an empty freedom, which did him more harm than good. His last recorded words sum up his chronically unstable character: 'So after all I never accomplished any heroic deeds. Yet I still long to distinguish myself—to reduce the whole world to dust, or gather together a gang of comrades to beat up Jews—it's all the same to me! I thought when I had cast off Matryona from my neck, now Grisha, you can swim away on your own, lift the anchor. . . . But I was born with unrest in my soul, and my fate is to be a tramp. I have wandered everywhere, but found no comfort. Of course I drink a lot. Vodka quenches the heart. As for towns, villages, people of different kinds, I find them all revolting!'

Gorky's early stories provide a gallery of original Russian types, apart from his celebrated tramps, although most of them share the tramp's deep craving to escape from ties of settled life and routine work. Such stories chronicle the God-forsaken provincial towns and villages which he visited, where men brawl and shout in vain attempts to dissipate their gnawing boredom. On a blank, empty face, even a scratch becomes a decoration. The more enterprising figures throw themselves into any reckless adventure which might stimulate their ossifying minds.

Ogip, the foreman in *The Icebreaker*, is romantically depicted as 'a leader of men', but what does his leadership amount to? He forces his sullen but obedient subordinates to follow him in the useless escapade of walking across a river on which the ice was breaking up. The alderman, in the story *Gubin*, inspires a blend of reverence and hatred because he has firmly decided that law and order must be hammered like nails into the people's vitals. In *The Saltmine* Gorky described from personal experience that kind of labour which cripples people mentally and physically, a stupefying labour from which any healthy individual will struggle to escape. Nor did he gloss over the brutal cynicism shown by his fellow workmen, who played a cruel practical joke on him.

Not all his early heroes are hardened men of action, reckless dreamers, or *tough guys*. Pure and gentle figures still appealed to him. His story *Nilushka* pictured the idiot son of a prostitute and a wandering monk. This frail lad with golden curls, like an angel in some ancient ikon, flitted about past mouldy huts and cracked fences, but his pathetic figure and incoherent words always brought comfort to the unfortunate people of the neighbourhood, who treated him with superstitious reverence and called him 'God's fool'. The story, *In the Steppe*, reveals the narrow margin which separates the tramp from the professional criminal. A wandering student and a soldier bound together by a common penury, find a fever-stricken carpenter lying helpless in the steppe. After the soldier has robbed the carpenter, the student goes one better, and coolly murders him, lest he should live to tell the tale against them.

Varenka Olesova (1897) stands apart as Gorky's only major story devoted to members of the professional and landowning class. It seems odd for Gorky to find a heroine among the noble-born landowners, but he was not then plagued by acute class-consciousness. He makes his beautiful and energetic Varenka tower above her own coarse peasants, and far above the conceited and sensual little botanist, Ippolit, who woos her. Ippolit persuades himself that he can help Varenka by trying to improve her untutored mind, while in reality he feels intoxicated by nothing but her magnificent body. But her integrity defeats him, even on his own intellectual ground, for she proves to have a strong and virtuously pagan soul, which brings her close in temperament to some of Gorky's vagabonds.

Varenka voiced one of Gorky's own persistent trains of thought. She complained that Russian novels bore her, because they lengthily repeat what she knows already, and are always too obviously true. They never help her to forget her everyday surroundings, as good novels ought to do. She dislikes reading heavy realistic stories about the peasants, because she learns nothing new. She knows her own peasants well enough, nor does she find them worthy of romantic treatment. Therefore she prefers French novels, because they invent brave adventurous heroes who stimulate her mind. She finds the educated Russian literary hero painfully stupid and clumsy. 'He is always sick of something, always thinking about something incomprehensible, feels sorry for everybody, but is himself a pathetic creature. And after he is married, he talks a lot of sour nonsense to his wife and then abandons her.' Like Gorky also, Varenka despised timid, petty slaves of orthodox convention and preferred impulsive criminals; she even confessed that her first and only love (a platonic one) was for a brave horse-thief captured in her father's village.

Through another character, the young Benkovsky, Gorky poured scorn on educated townsmen who knew the Russian countryside only in the guise of a holiday playground. 'Today, when every son of a peasant, merchant, or official, who has skimmed through a few popular booklets, calls himself a member of the intelligentsia—the real country can arouse no interest in them.'

Gorky skilfully disclosed how Ippolit began to understand his darker self by seeing his own image in his sister, and the manner in which she, like him, manipulated fine ideas in order to cloak and justify her cynical behaviour. 'Reason becomes most active and flexible, when a man needs to mask his feelings, and hide the coarse reality of his desires.' Ippolit lacked the strength to love Varenka, but secretly hoping to possess her, he persuaded himself that it was his duty to bring her education up to date.

People that once were Men (1897) provides a fitting end to Gorky's straightforward records of the tramps he knew. Men of all classes and conditions find their way *via* the tempting path of vagabondage into the same living grave, a doss-house run by the ex-cavalry officer, Konvalda. 'Women, shopkeepers, and philosophy,' he lucidly explains, 'have been the three causes of my ruin.' The ex-teacher admits that although he has talked a tremendous lot, it has done no good to anyone. 'The people are numberless, and I remain a stranger to them.' Obviously he, too, had read Nekrasov, whose final sentiments he echoed. A frustrated ex-inspector of schools dreamed of a new method of venting his accumulated malice against the world. 'I will go to America,' he announced, 'work my way up until I become President of the United States, and then I will challenge the whole of Europe to war and will blow it up.' These human wrecks still suffer, but their suffering leads to nothing more exalted than thoughts of self-annihilation. The grudge which they bear against the life they know turns into a feverish hatred against the whole world-order, a revolt against the last promptings of common sense. Though impotent and amorphous when left to their own devices, they could become demons of destruction in the hands of crafty leaders.

Indeed, Gorky soon found himself accused of encouraging potential bandits, and glorifying plain criminals, as if they were champions of wild justice against stupid man-made laws. After his impassioned protest against the massacre of Jews in Kishinev (1903), Burenin, leader-writer of the *New Times*, retaliated by writing bluntly that Gorky could not escape his major share of responsibility by trying to make the Government a scapegoat; because the men who carried out the brutal Kishinev pogrom had clearly been Gorky's own favourite heroes, Chelkashes, Konovalovs, and Grigory Orlovs. Evidently Gorky took this accusation very much to heart, for in all later editions of *The Orlov Couple* the inflammatory passage about beating up Jews was carefully omitted, and he repeatedly denounced anti-Semitism in many public declarations. He felt horrified that his lively picture of a Russian hooligan might serve to romanticize the Russian Government's vile treatment of its Jewish citizens.

IV

THE RETURN TO LEGEND

A TALENT which had blossomed in the savage Russian under-world could hardly be expected to provide an uplifting touch of ultimate harmony and release. Gorky excelled in wringing the reader's heart with painful or squalid scenes, drawn from experiences which more fastidious earlier writers had either passed over or treated with restraint. He faced his limitations honestly but tried to make the best of them. Since he could never hope to be another Pushkin or Turgenev, let him at least become a more vehement Belinsky or Reshetnikov, outraged but still undaunted; let his fierce indignant language stir up sluggish minds and rouse a purifying storm of anger in the battle against human brutality and smugness.

But before long an unforeseen obstacle obstructed him. He began to spoil his purer imaginative appeal by a wearisome spate of argument and strident denunciation. Disgust, however strongly felt, is negative, and demands some tangible relief to counterbalance it. Prolonged emotional floggings numbed the minds of those he hoped to rouse, until they reached the saturation point of apathy. 'Like hot tears falling on a cold and silent stone, my words no longer awake the smallest response in your hearts,' Gorky complained. He therefore conceived an ardent wish to embellish and adorn the ugly life which he had hitherto observed with piti-less truth. While his own most vivid stories pictured people whose main activity is anti-social and keenly destructive (*Chelkash*), or squandered uselessly in crazy escapades (*Foma Gordeyev*), he now longed to introduce active people of another kind, bursting with constructive talent, zeal, and buoyant *joie de vivre*. But since he knew no such people from experience, how could be create them out of nothing? 'Happiness is a desert island, inhabited entirely by creatures of my imagination,' one of his philosophic tramps remarked.

Long before he became a party propagandist, while still a *feuilleton* writer for the *Samara Gazette*, an imperative need to inject a vital stimulus into trite, matter-of-fact, modern literature preoccupied Gorky's mind. 'We live in a strange time of waning energy, of dim indifferent scepticism. It is our responsibility to correct all that, to make life blossom with fresh desires, to enrich it with our deeds, to ennoble thought by making it more reasonable, sane and varied' (*Samara Gazette*, 1895).

A little later, in 1900, Gorky told Chekhov that his consummate skill and mastery of detail was slaying the last relics of realism in literature. 'No one can go further than you in that direction.' After Chekhov's stories, all new stories seemed crude and clumsy, as though written not with a pen but with a cudgel. Yet Gorky said he felt none the less relieved that the topical, realistic school was ending, because the time had come when everybody needed a higher and more beautiful imaginative art than bare chronicles of prosaic modern life could ever hope to be. Very significant—but what did Gorky mean by this new edifying art? Certainly not the disembodied abstruse poetry of the Symbolist word-spinners (which he, like Tolstoy, plainly called degenerate), nor the weird, learned incantations of religious-minded intellectuals like Merezhkovsky, whom he detested, though both were then new movements, boosted by snobs and *avant-garde* critics, and coming into fashion.

On the contrary, Gorky sought the new stimulus in a wholehearted return to the almost forgotten wisdom of the past—neither in hazy brain-spun novelties, nor in sordid factual records of humdrum contemporary controversies, but in beautiful legends drawn from oral folk-lore which remote ancestors had handed down. It is evident that Gorky's so-called romantic figures from the Russian underworld were almost wholly drawn from life. His genuinely romantic or escapist strain, which tried to go beyond what he observed, developed on different lines. It started with elegant schematic moral parables (*The Siskin and the Wood-pecker* (1893), *The Song of the Falcon* (1895)), it went on more firmly and legitimately with a return to ancient folk-lore (*The Old Woman Iʒergil* (1895)). Even *Makar Chudra* was based on an oral tale from Bukovina, and *The Khan and his Son* bore the sub-title, *A Crimean Legend*. Gorky continued with uneasy efforts to re-discover ancient folk-lore heroes under the skins of modern revolutionary artisans (*Mother* (1907)). But in his last unfinished novel, *Klim Samgin* (1936), he reverted to the charm of unadulterated folk-legends in the figure of the old *diseuse* Fedosova, whose modest and radiant personality alone redeemed the blatant self-advertising modernity of the huge Nijni Novgorod trade fair.

Fedosova was over ninety when Gorky first saw her on the stage at Nijni Novgorod. Thirty thousand poems, songs, and legends had been written down from her amazing oral memory. Music and fairy-tales always stirred Gorky to the depths, and thirty years later he created his own remembered picture of Fedosova. As she moved forward, white-haired, wrinkled, tooth-less, with piercing eyes, there spread through the hall an atmo-sphere of ancient times. When she sang the song of a widow mourning for her husband, the spell-bound Klim Samgin 'could not take his eyes away from the play of wrinkles on that worn kindly face, from the strange brilliance of her child-like eyes, as she eloquently stressed every line of the verse she sang, and added to those weighty words a lively sparkle and a bewitching gentle rhythm'.

Gorky explained coherently his changing attitudes to folk-lore in the famous speech he made to the Moscow Writer's Congress in 1934. He had jumped to the conclusion that since oral folk-tales were invented by people who worked with their hands, there must be some mysterious link between manual labour and the gift of story-telling. Yet his attitude to labour remained throughout ambivalent. He was unable to exalt it in the theoretical manner of Marxian intellectuals, who had never held a spade in their hands, for he knew too much about its seamy side. He hardly stopped to think that the ancestors who first created folk-lore, ages before

III. Gorky and Chaliapin in the 1890s. From a photograph.

the days of giant factories and artificial nation-states, had worked in an environment poles apart from that of the Russian labourer in the late nineteenth century.

In his own wanderings, the drudgery of casual labour had exhausted him, less for its monotony than for its lack of sense. Yet he admitted that almost any manual work became a tonic when he felt intellectually confused and irritated. The perfunctory and dubious 'poetry of collective labour' belongs to his last phase of exhortation. But from his earliest days he admired efficient and creative effort, and mentally connected it with miraculous feats of legend, if only because it grew so rare in modern life, where greed for easy money was killing pride of work and skill in every class.

After helping stevedores to unload a cargo from a damaged barge in Kazan, he wrote: 'My soul kindled with the desire to spend the rest of my life in the half-mad ecstasy of doing things. . . . One felt like hugging and kissing those two-legged beasts, so clever and agile in their work, so self-forgettingly absorbed in it. It seemed that such joyously infuriated strength could overcome all obstacles and create miracles on earth, covering it in a single night with gorgeous palaces and cities, like one reads about in wise fairy-tales.' He never claimed, however, that the average modern artisan shared this imaginative enthusiasm for hard work, nor that the routine jobs of daily need could be organized by gambling on the maintenance of an ecstatic frame of mind.

The Old Woman Izergil, apart from the story of her own adventurous life, contains two ancient Bessarabian folk-tales which she told to Gorky. They reveal his inmost intellectual sympathies and his mastery of rhythmic prose. Gorky remembered the stories, which deeply impressed him, wrote them down for the first time, and probably embellished them, but, strictly speaking, they are not his creation. They are none the less remarkable for that. S. Aksakov had recorded in a similar way his old nurses' tale *The Little Scarlet Flower*, and so had Pushkin similar tales before him. All these re-told folk-stories owe their beauty to the language of a modern master.

Larra, in the story of that name, is the son of an eagle and a

D

human woman. A cold-blooded murderer, rigid in his cruelty and pride, he stood up against his judges, the human society in which he found himself. But, instead of condemning him to death, they devised for him a more terrible and painful punishment, complete freedom and the inability to die. So he steals and kills for ten years longer, and then, sick of life, he tries to kill himself. But even the sharpest dagger will not pierce his body. For many years he goes on wandering, racked with pain and loneliness, until he is worn away into an eternally moving shadow.

Gorky then asked the old woman to explain the strange bluish sparks which flicker across the Bessarabian steppes. 'Those sparks come from the burning heart of Danko,' she replied. 'An ancient story—you see how much happened in the past, and now there is nothing of the kind, neither deeds, nor people, nor stories like of old. If only you looked keenly enough into the past, you would be able to solve all your riddles. But you do not try to look, and therefore you can never learn how to live. I see every kind of person today, but there are no strong ones left among them. Where have they disappeared? And beautiful ones grow rarer every day.'

Like Larra, Danko stood alone, but unlike Larra, he had the friendliest intentions. He came not to exploit, destroy, or rule, but to save his fellow-creatures, to save them from wearing out their souls by yielding to their own sterile gloomy thoughts. He offered to lead these people out of the unhealthy swamp in which they lived, into a fertile land, invigorated by sunshine and pure air. They summed him up, saw that he was handsome, brave, and confident, and believed in him enough to follow him into the dark and terrifying forest. But after a time, as the forest grew denser, and they saw no end to it, they grew tired and angry, and started to mutter curses against their leader. And when he looked more closely at the people who surrounded him, he suddenly became aware that they were worse than beasts. He was giving his life to help them, but their faces showed no sign of gratitude or even sympathy, only cunning suspicion and cold hostility.

Though his heart flared up with indignation, pity for the people soon extinguished it. He had been devoted to them, and he thought again that without him they would perish. So his heart began to burn with the desire to save them. They, watching him like wolves, expected that he wanted to escape from them, and hemmed him in on every side, in order to seize and kill him. He read their thoughts. Then suddenly he tore open his chest, pulled out his own heart, and held it high over his head. It flamed brighter than the sun and lit up the path. The forest opened up, and the amazed crowd, wild with excitement, rushed forward to find their promised land. They did not even notice Danko's death, nor that his heart was still aflame beside the prostrate corpse. Then one frightened man turned aside and kicked it angrily, so that it flew asunder in a multitude of sparks.

This legend fails to fit in neatly with current Soviet interpretations of Gorky's folk-lore. Even the best indoctrinated critics have not tried to prove that it presented a gratifying picture of the part played by revolutionary masses on the march. And they refrain from comment on the fate of bold reformers who would rather die for their beliefs than promote their advancement by false promises, or by yielding to the frenzied passions of a mob. Also how dangerously unorthodox that one good man, by his voluntary sacrifice, should save so many less attractive fellow-creatures.

Despite all this inherent testimony to the contrary, some Soviet critics have perfunctorily pointed to Danko as a symbol of the budding Bolshevik. Nor can they be blamed for that special pleading, since Gorky tried to do the same in building up one of his most artificial heroes, Pavel in the novel *Mother*. For readers less mentally entangled, however, Gorky's early fairy-tales remain rich in a rather cruel integrity and picturesque charm of language, whereas his later hybrid blend of moralizing fairy-tale and contemporary fact is marred by clumsy partisan argument and blatantly incompatible intentions. Gorky never seems to have learned that it is useless to argue with those whom no argument will convince.

V

THE CHOICE OF ALLIES

THE second phase of Gorky's literary work revealed the heavy imprint on his mind of unremitting social pressure. Like every successful Russian writer, he was forced to feel that his natural author's duty to improve his art must surrender to an outside task-master, the endlessly debated *service of society*, as interpreted by its self-appointed guardians. After his first volume of stories had appeared, the public clamoured for the next instalment, and the critics demanded edifying and topical work. He arrived on the scene when the giants were leaving it, at a moment when imaginative literature was merging either with ephemeral journalistic sketches or bald social pamphleteering, when even the mighty Tolstoy had turned into a cold and dreary preacher, and disenchanted *narodniks*, like Gleb Uspensky, were spreading a mood of sterility and self-pitying impotence.

Gorky's early stories carried no clear-cut moral teaching. Indeed their sheer vitality and shockingly *amoral* tone appealed to readers tired of chewing the old moral cud. But though he sprang to fame without the topical social message, obstinately demanded by all 'progressive' intellectuals since Chernyshevsky, he still found himself dependent for professional progress and popularity on the favour of two rival groups of publicists. Neither the established *narodniks*, nor their Marxian rivals, gave him a moment's peace, and they forced him to choose between them. Each courted and needed him to serve their own political campaigns. Instinctively aware of this predicament, Gorky was in no hurry to be pinned down, and long after he had taken sides, he still repeated that in every group and party he always regarded himself as a heretic. He clung to his precarious independence while he could, and to start with, he preferred the more palpably Russian *narodnik* appeal to the dry 'scientific' logic of the Westernized Marxians.

'My sympathies lay on the side of those *preservers*, eccentric people, but extraordinarily pure in heart. Their social ideals carried me away, although I found them comic heroes.' The mystic invocation of Gleb Uspensky's popular novel, *The Power of the Earth*, pictured the long-suffering Russian peasant bearing on his stalwart shoulders the whole frightful burden of the Russian state. So long as he was a tiller of the soil, so long as the power of the earth ruled over him, he would remain patient, strong, and young in soul. But the peasant who contemptuously abandoned his own mother-earth, and migrated to the towns in search of material ease and higher wages, would be doomed to degenerate into a drunkard or a callous criminal.

That novel managed to convey a certain sombre moral grandeur. It testified to the human misery and squalor inflicted by uncontrolled industrialization and hectic personal greed, and it gripped the minds of idealists who believed that Russia might still escape from being sucked into the degrading industrial whirlpool of the West. But it was demonstrably *Utopian*, if understood in that literal, dry, and nakedly practical sense, which was all that radical readers were accustomed to extract from imaginative novels. The average Russian peasant was, in fact, shrewd and cunning. He was rarely a gentle suffering martyr. It was purely a noble act of art for a generous-minded novelist to see him in that light. And whether or not the cultured reader deplored the moral corruption brought by mechanized industry and lust for money, he began to see that even agriculture must be scientifically mechanized, if the too rapidly growing Russian peasant population was not to starve.

Tolstoy himself, as an active landlord, who invested large sums of money in improving his own estates, buying pedigree stock, etc., obviously recognized this truth in practice, although in unguarded moments of uncompromising later *Tolstoyan* doctrine, he came dangerously close to Gleb Uspensky. For the agrarian idealist (usually ignorant of science) the approaching agricultural

paradise would emerge in a friendly agglomeration of co-opera-
tives, hazily reconciling experiments of the new independent
peasant and the working landowner with the stagnant peasant
commune.

For a time Gorky fully succumbed to the *narodnik* spell, talked
about founding an agricultural colony himself together 'with two
telegraphists and a nice young lady', and even wrote a letter to
Tolstoy asking to be presented *gratis* with a piece of his un-
cultivated land. In 1889 he called at Tolstoy's house in Moscow,
but failed to find him at home. Countess Tolstoy none the less
gave him a meal in the kitchen, and took the opportunity to lecture him severely about the many worthless idlers who sponged
on Tolstoy's misguided charity. That particular infatuation ended
abruptly after a talk with the *narodnik* writer, Karonin, who had
recently endured the torments of a volunteer agricultural colony,
which had petered out in personal rancour and hopelessly hap-
hazard business management. Though Gorky continued to admire
individual *narodniks* who were ready to endure exile in Siberia and
suffer for their faith, he soon concluded that their muddled agricultural exploits, and the unbalanced thwarted misfits to whom
they principally appealed, entirely failed to stand the test of real
contemporary application and economic sanity.

Moreover the clear-sighted Korolenko, who is usually labelled
a *narodnik*, without proper qualification, had developed into a
merciless critic of *narodnik* fallacies and abuses. He not only encouraged Gorky, but as an elder statesman in the literary world,
he helped considerably to guide him. Many contemporary
searchers after truth, he told him, whether unconventional tramps
or restless characters in fiction, were no better than idlers and
malicious scoundrels. 'What they are really searching for is
nothing more sacred than an easy living at the expense of some-
one else.'[1] He also told Gorky his sceptical forecast that the crass
materialists would soon become the ruling fashion, because they
would seduce all discontented people by the novel simplicity of
their doctrine, most of all people who had grown too lazy to

[1] A. Volkov, *M. Gorky*, p. 48, Moscow, 1951.

think for themselves. As a literary connoisseur, he counselled Gorky to indulge less in turgid melodramatic language. 'I doubt whether that romantic Lazarus, who died long ago, is worthy of resurrection. It seems to me that you do not sing enough with your own voice.'[1]

A glance at the dead-end 'social' literature of the eighteen-eighties is enough to explain the disenchantment of Gorky and Korolenko. In Albov's story, *The Day of Reckoning*, 'the aspirations of an eagle allied with the strength of a ladybird' lead the self-tortured hero to a suicide which can only be welcomed as a merciful release. Gleb Uspensky's last published sketches, *Willy Nilly*, depict with a touch of exasperated humour a young intellectual of indefinite occupation and means, blown hither and thither by the winds of chance. He settled in a village, talked endlessly about making a parliamentary constitution for the Russian Empire, drank a lot of tea, sitting round a table together with a gloomy student and a gloomy midwife. After two years his friend from St. Petersburg revisited him, found him engaged in exactly the same talk and tea-drinking, except that the party had recently been joined at the table by an eloquent member of the *Zemstvo*;[2] the phrase, 'I am stifled', was frequently repeated.

One of Potapenko's popular novels belonging to this period was pointedly entitled *Not a Hero*. The way was clear for Garshin and the poet Nadson to revel in the shattered aspirations of lofty souls, and in the contemplation of exhausted strength alleviated by tenuous day-dreams. 'The end of the eighties and the beginning of the nineties can be called years spent in justifying weakness and consoling people already condemned to be destroyed,' Gorky harshly summed up later.

The professional classes lived more quietly than before, since after the events of 1881 active protest was ruled out. But plain statistics showed how many gallons of vodka were drunk, how many people went mad. Gorky impressed the reading public because he reacted whole-heartedly against this autumnal atmosphere of creeping self-extinction, a mood for which the minor

[1] A. Volkov, *M. Gorky*, p. 48, Moscow, 1951.   [2] Local government council.

narodnik writers were partially responsible. He also pointed out their major blunders. They tried to ram the complicated teachings of Herbert Spencer and Mikhailovsky down the throats of simple people who merely wanted to own a little cultivable land, and were not a bit interested in the part to be played by personalities in the unfolding historical process. Some of these writers he also found personally vain and spiteful. He observed how in their glowing speeches about self-sacrifice and wider social justice their eyes only started to glitter when they got the better of an opponent in a verbal battle.

He felt more and more frustrated and ill at ease in the company of such heartless hypocrites. Yet he hesitated before impulsively consigning the whole intelligentsia to the devil. The masses were still sheep without a shepherd. His respected friend Korolenko had convinced him that individuals of outstanding mental gifts and firm character provided the sole reliable guarantee of any wider social improvement. Korolenko had compared Socrates and Giordano Bruno to their own line of Russian intellectual martyrs, to the gallant Decembrists and the heroic regicides, Sofia Perovskaya and Zelyabov. Such leaders set a fine example, even though their would-be followers had dragged it in the mud. They were guiding stars who still had light to give. For the sticky bog of fashionable mediocrity had not yet sucked them down.

Finally, recognizing that powerful intellectual allies were indispensable to keep him going, Gorky decided to form a working compact with what seemed to be the rising group, the Marxian socialists, and sacrificed his earlier loyalty to the *narodniks*. Though he remarked to Vladimir Posse that Marxism 'lowered one's individuality', he conquered his spiritual misgivings, and in 1897 he joined the editorial board of the Social Democratic periodical, *Jizn*. In an attempt to dispel his doubts, he explained to Chekhov that *Jizn* aimed at a harmonious blend of *narodnik* teaching with Marxism, but at the same time he innocently admitted, 'I understand nothing about this kind of thing.'

Personal factors contributed a lot to Gorky's choice. The friendly efforts of the left-wing journalist, Posse, had induced

The Literary Fund to give him an urgently needed eight hundred roubles which enabled him to pay for a cure in the Crimea. More important still, after all negotiations with established publishing houses had failed, it was the dogged perseverance of two social democrats, Dorovatovsky and Charushnikov, that secured the eventual publication of the first two volumes of Gorky's *Stories and Sketches* (1898). While their social doctrines meant little to him, the generous strain in his nature responded to timely and valuable help from individuals who believed in him.

VI

THE ESTABLISHED AUTHOR AS A SOCIAL TEACHER

THE Russian reading public greeted these first two volumes of collected stories with such tempestuous enthusiasm that within a year a second edition appeared, and simultaneously a new third volume. All three volumes were quickly reprinted and began to sell in tens of thousands. The name of Gorky became a household word throughout the Russian Empire. Pictures of the fascinating ex-tramp appeared on postcards, cigarette boxes, and a multitude of advertisements.

Gorky was well on his way to becoming the nineteenth-century equivalent of a contemporary television *celebrity*, record-breaking athlete, or Hollywood film-star. But he showed his character both by a firm dislike of vulgar and easy notoriety, and by spending a very small amount of his big literary earnings on himself. Popular success neither corrupted him nor turned his head, although it emboldened him to be more harshly outspoken on appropriate occasions. He wrote to Andreyev: 'The praise of the Russian man in the street, who habitually bribes everyone, from the policeman to God, is suspect' (Letter, 1902). Far from grovelling to his mass admirers, he felt freer to tell them unpalatable truths.

When in 1901 he attended the first performance of Chekhov's *Uncle Vanya* at the Moscow Art Theatre, the public came crowding round him in the interval. But instead of bowing or smiling to them, he turned and addressed them reproachfully: 'Why do you keep staring at me?' he said. 'I am not the Venus of Medici, nor a ballerina, nor a drowned man. What can you find of interest in the physical exterior of a man who writes stories? Go and watch Chekhov's magnificent play, but don't waste the interlude in trivialities.'[1] The daily Press made a scandal story from this incident. The illustrated papers revelled in caricatures of Gorky, with his sad spaniel eyes and fierce walrus moustache, poised in a very inappropriate ballet skirt. And he gained an extra name for gratuitous boorishness. But being a hardened journalist himself, he took what notoriety came to him without undue concern. In his sketch, *About the Author who gave himself Airs*,[2] he warned the commercially successful author against allowing himself to get 'stuck in the slough of popularity', and explained that the public is less likely to praise him for any genuine merits than because he provides their jaded appetite with some sharp and poignant new sensation. For the public, he wrote sardonically, 'you are like a young mistress taken by a worn-out old man'.

Perhaps Gorky secretly basked in the public admiration which he affected to despise, and he seems to have behaved differently in private meetings with his closer friends. Then he would shed his booming bass voice, and boorish swagger, and talk almost apologetically, in a gentle joking tone, modest to the verge of self-effacement. At any rate, he could play both parts convincingly.

Nor should we conclude that Gorky's initial wave of almost hysterical popularity, however sweeping, continued for long unimpeded. It horrified some thoughtful critics from the start, though their protesting voices were concerned, less with Gorky's appeal to cultured people, who admired his writings with mature detachment, than with his harmful effect on the average reader's crude, impressionable, unguarded mind. Suvorin's *Novoe Vremya* admitted that he had strong qualities of his own, but accused him of having absorbed the worst defects of the half-educated class which he attacked. While the older *narodnik* writers at least had tried to discover a man in the beast, it complained, Gorky had singled out the beast in man. 'So long as a beast is young, vigorous, and insensitive, all Gorky's sympathies are on the side of the beast.' Another critic, M. Moskal, published a whole book

---

[1] V. Rusakov, *M. Gorky*, p. 12, Moscow, 1903.
[2] *Sobranniye Sochineniy*, vol. 5, p. 306, Moscow.

to prove that Gorky's evil writings were a menace to society, because they glorified hooligans in no uncertain terms. 'Hooligans are his only heroes, and most of them are psychopaths. . . .' He creates pathos out of brooding melancholy and a craving for indefinite things.[1]

In 1901 Gorky was arrested, accused of various revolutionary activities, and confined in the Nijni Novgorod prison. The arrest took place after the publication of that issue of *Jizn* which contained his melodramatic rebellious allegory, *The Stormy Petrel*. In April an administrative order suspended the publication of *Jizn*. Gorky himself fared better. Thanks to Tolstoy's generous intercession on his behalf, he was released within a month. But from now on the police pried more persistently into all his activities.

In 1902 the Imperial Academy of Sciences elected him a member, and Nicholas II, indignant at the impropriety of their choice, ordered them to cancel the election. Korolenko and Chekhov both protested against Gorky's exclusion and resigned from the Academy themselves. Tolstoy, who attached little importance to the Academy, took no action, convinced that the arts could never be healthily promoted by any official institutions. He seems to have shared the attitude of the influential critic, V. Stasov, who wrote at the time: 'I am by no means a disciple of Gorky, and it interests me very little whether he is made an Academician or not. Who the devil needs Academies? But I simply did not like the way they treated him.' Publicity about this incident, and the Government's mild but irritating persecution of Gorky served only to defeat the Government's main purpose. Instead of suppressing Gorky, it enhanced his established fame and bound him more closely to his revolutionary friends.

On the whole the Government's treatment of Gorky, though clumsy and arbitrary, was humane. Suffering already from tuberculosis, he sent a petition from Arzamas, where he was exiled, for permission to travel to the Crimea for medical treatment. The Government soon granted his petition, and after being allowed to

---

[1] M. Moskal, *Opravdanie Zla.*, St. Petersburg, 1902.

IV. Scene from the first Moscow Art Theatre production of *The Lower Depths* (1901). In centre, Stanislavsky in the role of *Satin*.

attend a riotous farewell banquet in Nijni Novgorod, he departed for the sunny south. In April 1902 his permit expired, and he was obliged to return to Arzamas.

In 1890 Gorky had married Ekaterina Voljina, a proof-reader on the *Samara Gazette*. The marriage did not turn out to be a happy or a lasting one, though he remained on friendly terms with his wife after they had separated. For a man so vehemently unrestrained in all his public utterances, he was fastidiously reticent about his private life, as if he had determined to keep all intimate secrets permanently hidden from the *evil eye* of public scrutiny. Only a few passages in letters to Chekhov lift the veil a little, and they reveal sentiments remote from that militant social optimism which he cultivated so assiduously to impress the outside world. In 1899 he wrote to him: 'I should like to be absolutely alone, even more alone than you are. A family may be a good thing, but you do better not to have any.' [1]

His visit to Petersburg that year, to meet celebrities of the literary world, he described as a nightmare, stupidly unpleasant and absurd. In the same year he wrote that a young prostitute, whom he had 'saved', and allowed to live in his house, had created a family melodrama by spreading rumours that she lived in intimate relations with him. He suggested to Chekhov that they should travel together to China. When he heard that Chekhov was about to marry the Moscow actress, Olga Knipper, he wrote in surprise: 'I hesitate to believe it. But if it is true, then I am happy. It is good to be married if your wife is not made of wood and has no radical ideas. But children are best of all.' [2]

After his return to Arzamas in 1902 he complained of his sombre moral state, irritability, and boredom. He wrote to Chekhov: 'If I am not allowed to leave here in the autumn, I shall fall in love with the tax-inspector's housekeeper. I shall pull her up to the top of the highest belfry, and then I shall throw myself down—with her of course. The Press will announce the tragic death of Maxim Gorky. . . . The dogs howl, the crows croak, the

[1] G. Aleksinsky, *La Vie Amère de Maxim Gorky*, p. 111, Paris, 1950.
[2] *M. Gorky i A. Chekhov, Perepiska*, p. 48, Moscow–Leningrad, 1937.

cocks crow, the bells ring; as for men, there are none. Priests roam the streets in search of somebody to bury. . . . The tax-inspector's housekeeper is the only attractive woman among the ten thousand inhabitants of our town, but this she-devil serves love with so much zeal that her admirers will surely tear her to pieces, or else Venus will remove her nose.'[1]

Much Soviet ink has been used in demonstrating from his Tsarist police records, at this period and earlier, how fiercely and consistently revolutionary Gorky had been. While nobody would dispute that he was a born 'stormy petrel', we are by now aware how normal and natural it was for leading Russian writers to be spiritual rebels, even when they differed widely in the degree to which they were involved in current political and public agita-tion. Gorky's *narodnik* friends, though often admirable people, had not turned out to be the salt of the earth, nor had they per-ceptibly helped society by their rather muddle-headed teaching. The Marxian revolutionaries, who stepped into their shoes, said, among other things—smash the evil power of the modern nation-state, so that the ablest men may start to lead its ignorant citizens.

That was the deceptively simple call to action, which appealed to Gorky's impulsive nature as a stimulating alternative to the frustration endured under *non-violent* methods. What a blessed economy of effort to find a single scapegoat, and to identify the stuffy autocratic state with the arch-enemy of Russian welfare.

Thus, after long sharing Korolenko's concern for a slow deter-mined, but legal course of action, Gorky began to support every action or party, legal or illegal, which might help to overthrow the Government autocracy. It was natural that he should mix more with well-meaning artisans and idealistic students, who dabbled in conspiracy and plots. In any case the detailed account of his political activities, such as they were, can safely be left to Soviet commentators, who are naturally attracted to make the most of this subject, and who have access to the only docu-mentary sources.

[1] G. Aleksinsky, *La Vie Amère de Maxim Gorky*, p. 114, Paris, 1950.

Nevertheless, his most thorough and fair-minded biographer, and one-time personal friend, has stated: 'Gorky told me definitely that he never belonged to any political party. In the revolutionary movement he was merely a sympathizer, though to be sure, a very active one.'[1] There can be no doubt that Gorky always sympathized with individuals whom he admired, rather than with political parties to which they happened to belong. Even among the parties favoured by him, he included Social Revolutionaries as well as Bolsheviks and Mensheviks, much to the annoyance of those who aspired to be the sole exploiters of his talent, fame, and substantial literary earnings. At times he called himself a social democrat, and he undoubtedly preferred the vigorous opportunism of Lenin to the more doctrinaire or devious tactics of other would-be political leaders. But, as late as 1911, eight years after the official split in the Social Democratic Party, he was still urging Bolsheviks and Mensheviks to re-unite, so that Lenin had to remind him bluntly that this was a hopeless project.

A more lasting and lucrative venture than the political periodical, *Jizn*, came with the enterprising foundation of the *Znanie* publishing house (1901), a co-operative in which all participating authors held shares and took the profit on their own publications. It started well, though eventually it petered out through internecine feuds, until Gorky and Pyatnitsky remained the sole surviving shareholders. And in the end Pyatnitsky swindled Gorky. Far from being jealous of other talented young writers, Gorky sought them out with more generous discrimination than he is usually given credit for. His own name, plus the contributions of members like Veresayev, Bunin, Kuprin, and Chirikov, soon made *Znanie* a serious rival to the older commercial publishing houses of imaginative literature. By launching out into occasional miscellanies, publishing the work of first-class contemporary foreign writers, including Walt Whitman, Knut Hamsun, and Emile Verhaeren, *Znanie* also struck the note of broad international European culture which the more enlightened Russian reading public then demanded.

[1] A. Kaun, *M. Gorky*, p. 407.

Both Chekhov and Nemirovich-Danchenko had for some time been coaxing Gorky to try his hand in a new medium and to write a play for the recently-founded Moscow Art Theatre. During his enforced stay in Arzamas, he responded by *The Philistines*, a sprawling mediocre work, but staged in 1901 with moderate success. Soon afterwards he completed the one play by which he is chiefly remembered, a sociological drama called *The Lower Depths*. From its first production in December 1901 it aroused wild enthusiasm.

Readers should recall that the play's triumph with the Moscow public owed a lot to the mastery with which it was interpreted by Stanislavsky and the superb actors of the Moscow Art Theatre. Gorky admitted this, and frankly said that Kachalov, in the part of the Baron, created something 'far greater than what I wrote'. But it proved equally successful when performed by German actors in Berlin. And even in its printed form the play became a best-seller and ran through fourteen editions in one year (1903). Its concentration on the current vogue for vagabonds, and the shock of brutal novelty, no doubt added spice to its popular appeal. Never before had so much human riff-raff been represented on the stage in all its grim and naked squalor, rags, and dirt. Not for nothing had the Art Theatre actors spent hours *incognito* sitting in Moscow doss-houses, watching the inmates' behaviour and taking copious notes.

The glamour and excitement of *The Lower Depths* have faded since burglars, murderers, and prostitutes have become stage commonplaces, and objects of daily familiarity throughout the newspaper-reading world. Indeed the 'dust-bin dramatist' of today has outdone Gorky. Not content with kneeling in the mud, he grovels in the gutter, and swears that it is higher than the stars. Gorky himself later described his play as out-of-date, 'even harmful in our time'. But though it has worn and dated in some ways, it remains important as the swan-song of the thoughtful vagabond, and Gorky's most ambitious attempt to extract a coherent philosophy of action from the well-worn vagabond theme. The two fullest characters, whose juxtaposition makes the substance of the play, are Luka, the wandering teacher, and Satin, the unjustly treated criminal.

Gorky intended to contrast favourably the strong-minded murderer, who will stop at nothing to get his sweet revenge, with the elusive soothing old man who tries to comfort every suffering person. Yet Luka remains an enigmatic character, who makes no distinctly black or white impression, the more so since he is seen chiefly through the eyes of other characters, who all judge him differently. In the acted play Luka came out so creditably that Gorky later complained to Lunacharsky that the actor, Moskvin, by taking Luka too seriously, had ennobled him out of all proportion to his merits.

According to Gorky, Luka should have been a sly old fellow, who had become soft and pliable through having been knocked about a lot. He poked his nose into other people's affairs, scattered his sympathy too lavishly in all directions, failed to discriminate between the deserving and the undeserving. 'I respect scoundrels too,' he says; 'In my opinion not a single flea is bad; they are all black and they all jump.' Luka's rule of conduct was that men wanted to forget hard facts and to be consoled; they had no need of truths which did not help them. If truths were so painful that they destroyed self-confidence, let them remain concealed.

In a technical sense Satin is a murderer, for we are told that he killed a man who tried to violate his sister. A crime committed in such extenuating circumstances would in most countries be punished leniently. But in this play Satin has spent three years in prison, and after his release he remains a social pariah; all paths are closed to him. This improbable harshness somewhat weakens the convincing quality of Satin, but he remains an intelligent and even chivalrous personality. He defends his rival Luka from spiteful slander, only because worse people, like the contemptible Baron, have abused him. He recognizes that Luka is a liar, justified by excellent intentions, but he is not content to follow Luka's example. 'Of course he lies, but it is out of pity for you, devil take you! . . . Weak people, and those who live on other people's energy, they need a lie. . . . Some are supported by it, others it

E

serves as a disguise. Only a man who is master of himself, what need has he of lies? Lies form the religion both of slaves and masters. . . . Truth is the God of the free man!'

Satin impulsively agrees with Luka's prescription for better living, and concludes that if a super-carpenter appears, more skilful than any ever seen on earth before, the ordinary workaday carpenters will all admire him and try to emulate his wonderful example. Blissfully ignorant of trade-union morality, he never considers that they may feel more like murdering a super-carpenter, who puts them all to shame. Satin achieved his philosophic climax with the long bombastic speech which he pronounced prior to the actor's suicide at the end of the play. It starts: 'Everything pleases me when I am drunk'; and it ends in a dithyrambic glorification of the human race. 'Everything is in man and for him. He alone exists—everything else is the work of his hands and brain. . . . *Man*—that sounds proud, one must respect man and not humiliate him with pity. . . . I always despised people who worry too much about filling their stomachs. Man is much higher than a full stomach.'

- Some Russian critics glorify this speech as a fair specimen of what they call Gorky's optimistic humanism. To others, but especially to non-Russian minds, it is more remarkable as a symptom, a dramatic warning of the disastrous way in which half-educated men can become intoxicated by treacherous and empty slogans. Here a monstrous colourless abstract *man* envelops and obliterates the variegated human being of flesh and blood. 'It is neither you, me, nor them,' Satin raves; 'It is you, they, the old man, Napoleon, Mahomet. . . . All in one!' And the figure of a man which Satin sketches in the empty air with his finger as he pronounces these wild words is an appropriate symbol of that vague, soulless, but grotesquely conceited ethic, which harassed and puzzled Gorky even when he tried so hard to instil it into the minds of his admiring audience.

A philosophic play in which pathetically degraded characters, who have lost the shape of normal men, begin to idolize their own sick fancies of *ideal* men, is bound to jar through lack of sanity and measure. Changes of mood are too abrupt and arbitrary. At one moment men are frankly compared with vermin; ugly brutes and far too numerous, they breed indiscriminately, encumber and spoil the earth, where they 'crawl like cockroaches'. Then in a brighter interval the same nasty creatures change suddenly into God-like lords of creation, and arrogantly pronounce themselves to stand above the laws of nature.

While this concluding speech of Satin may flow appropriately from the mouth of a thoughtful ex-convict in an expansive mood, we are hardly entitled to tear it from the context and present it as Gorky's own considered philosophic message. His central theme remained the disparity between factual truth and inspiring legend, and the human need for both. To make it a moving drama, Gorky needed Luka as much as Satin. He floundered in the mental conflict between them because he would never admit that faith and logic can belong to separate spheres. Where legend reveals a spiritual faith it need not *lie*, provided it makes no logical statement about verifiable facts, but goes outside them. Like a beautiful thing it can help people most by being simply what it is.

Yet Gorky remained perpetually oppressed by the petty factual truths which (isolated from any faith) drip on a man's head like water in a Chinese torture, and slowly crush his will-power. Therefore he set out to justify not merely an unverifiable legend, but even a 'helpful lie', however demonstrably false, so long as either could revive the flagging will to live.

This went a step further than before in setting up the biggest and most brazen lies as desirable instruments for controlling human action. For the old lament which Pushkin voiced about the destructiveness of 'low truths' and the benefit of 'elevating deceptions', turned out wrong, if one admitted tiny atomic truths of fact, and a separate order of spiritual truths. The latter, whether elevating or not, could never be mere *deceptions* so long as they bore no logical reference to truths of fact. But such a sober limitation could never satisfy Gorky's intellectual arrogance.

Nevertheless we must admit that his recurrent apologia for the 'helpful lie' matured effectively in the character of Luka, to whom it remained a responsibility of personal discretion. At least Luka brought comfort to the dying Anna by his affection and sympathetic words, when that was what she needed, and nothing else could help her. He talked to her kindly about an after-life in a language that she could understand, even if he disbelieved in it himself. And he revived in the desperate drunken actor a hope that he might still be cured, although he knew him to be incurable. He thus concealed factual truths from people on whom they might have weighed too heavily to be bearable. But he could equally tell the plain unvarnished truth when it was needed, and serve the same helpful motive as when he lied. He warned the thief, Pepel, against the diabolical woman, Vasilissa, who wanted him to murder her own husband. He told the timid Natasha not to be afraid of ghosts, but to be on guard against the living enemies around her. If Gorky intended Satin to portray a more advanced and *socially useful* personality than Luka, perhaps the *Art Theatre* actors were instinctively in the right when they reversed the emphasis. With all Satin's ecstatic eloquence about his imaginary abstract man, he seems to have brought less temporary pleasure or material improvement to any real person whom he met.

The Lower Depths, apart from being Gorky's philosophic swan-song of the social outcast, bore witness to new creative stirrings in his mind. His best earlier stories had thrown a high-light on strong and self-reliant characters at loggerheads with their drab environment, by no means only tramps, but also princes, landowners, and legendary figures (*The Khan and his Son, Varenka Olesova, The Burning Heart*). Together with a revolt against classic resignation to the stern decrees of fate, the Promethean Danko, the proud Malva, who will not submit to any man, the wounded falcon who, still struggling to fly, falls to his death on the rocks (*The Song of the Falcon*, 1895), they all show the same indomitable lust for a life worth dying for.

While he had neither morally whitewashed nor tried to rationalize their unpredictable, impulsive conduct, he was clearly fascinated by their integrity, by their refusal to be dragged down by convention-bound society. After all these glowing pictures of buoyant, energetic men and women, Gorky changed over paradoxically to an apologia for weak or broken individuals. Sometimes they are the same people as before, seen at a later stage of life. The characters in *The Lower Depths* have all started boldly, and then been broken on the wheel. But Gorky could more easily start to justify sympathetic but defeated people, because some of his favourite heroes had been men of quite ordinary capacities, struggling to play gigantic roles beyond their strength. It was inevitable that many of his defiant tramps and ultra-individual misfits, if they could not die bravely before their youthful vigour was exhausted, should sink into the dull abasement of the doss-house.

VII

AN OBSERVER OF THE NEW
INDUSTRIAL CLASS

MEANWHILE a new section of his environment began to claim Gorky's keen attention. The merchants of the Volga towns had hailed his spectacular success. These self-made *nouveau-riches* felt justly proud of him, a local product of their own Nijni Novgorod, like them a self-made man. They made him welcome in their lavishly hospitable homes. Gorky became aware again that the Volga region remained his permanent spiritual background. This flourishing merchant class, which now admitted him as an honoured equal, showed a breezy constructive vigour, wholly absent from the decaying small tradespeople he had known in his poverty-stricken childhood. He began to watch them closely and to reflect on their significant complexity. *Foma Gordeyev* (1898) is the first of his novels devoted to this Russian merchant *milieu* as it appeared to him at the turn of the last century.

This novel marks a striking transfer, not only in social setting, but still more in personal sympathy. The *strong* characters, instead of being irresponsible or anti-social dare-devils as before, are now exactly the reverse; they have become active, calculating, and successful business-men. The weaklings (or rather those who aspire to deeds beyond their strength) spring from the younger generation of the same class, who struggle to escape from bondage to their own parents, the ruling merchants and financiers. Gorky clearly felt a thrill of admiration for the strong self-made Ignat, Foma's father. Both the old-fashioned Anany Shchuryov and the bold *entrepreneur*, Mayakin, fascinated him. Yet the burden of his sympathy falls on Foma, the latest human product of these vital merchants, who after rebelling against them all, is finally crushed by their overwhelming *system* and defensive sense of social solidarity. His cry of protest against the cunning, self-satisfied Mayakin is Gorky's own familiar outcry. 'Oh, you swine, what have you created? Not a new life and order, but a prison where you fasten human beings in chains. It's stifling, cramped, you have left no place for a living soul to turn. You're soul-destroyers. . . . Don't you understand, it's only on account of human endurance that you're still left alive?'

Foma's godfather, Mayakin (against whom this invective strikes), is the most modern and managerial of all Gorky's merchant types. An intellectual business man who believes in machinery as the main source of the *entrepreneur*'s power over his employees, he promotes the rational levelling down of every human being to his specific function in the service of the industrial state. No flattering hypocrisy of humane benevolence masks his attitude to the average workman. They should all work in the sphere where they belong by their capacities. 'Calves have no business to growl like bears;' he remarks. Psychologically Mayakin bears a striking resemblance to his immediate successors on the industrial scene, the Bolshevik boss and party technician. Like Lenin, he expressed his firm conviction that the strongest economic organization or class must also win and wield political power. 'What is the good of having money if it does not lead to power?' he asked. And for him the state remained the natural organ of every ruling class. He even affirmed: 'When the state is able to inspire all its citizens with a single opinion, compels everyone to think alike, that is beautiful and wise.' And, like Stalin, he justified the ambitions of plebeian industrial dictators by finding ample precedents in Russian history. 'For centuries we merchants and trading people have really carried Russia on our own shoulders. We still do so. Peter the Great, a Tsar of divine wisdom, recognized our worth and supported us. But now we stand on our own feet.'

In other ways Mayakin resembles Dostoyevky's *Grand Inquisitor*, applying his talents to build up industrial organization.

He sets out to rule deliberately by cunning and deceit because no other methods have yet proved workable, and he favours giving foolish people enough rope with which to hang themselves. 'If the time comes when every nincompoop imagines he can do everything—then give the rascal freedom. He will puff himself out in all directions, until, poor creature, he will dissipate his strength. Then worthier people will gain the upper hand, real statesmen who will know how to direct life, not with a cudgel or with a pen, but with their strong hands and brains.' Mayakin characteristically compares human beings to bricks which must be made according to the exact dimensions specified by a master-builder. Thus every man becomes a piece of capital to be exploited solely for the profit of the state, down to his last sinew. He is simply a part of the state's capital investment, and must produce a corresponding dividend.

But Gorky is equally at pains to demonstrate that the merchant class is far from uniform. In contrast to Mayakin, he sets Anany Shchuryov, a lumber merchant of the older school, who, unlike Mayakin, has come to the conclusion that modern machinery is a trap set by the devil to catch human beings and break their spirit. For him, the unaccustomed luxury and ease provided by labour-saving machines, saps the human will to work, and turns men into vicious lazybones or dull-witted oafs. Anany is no patriarchal simpleton sighing for the past, for he also shows a sinister and contradictory streak. The thoughtful seer who talked so edifyingly about God, and the pitiless harsh merchant who crushed his business rivals, are two distinct unrelated personalities inhabiting one and the same man. And while his calm blue eyes looked wise and virtuous, his horribly gross and sensual lips told another story.

Among all these vigorous merchant characters, Gorky seems to find most satisfaction in depicting Foma's father, Ignat. The beginning of the novel, devoted mainly to his biography, provides about the best constructed consecutive chapters Gorky ever wrote. Ignat is built in the heroic mould of a folk-tale *bogatyr*. He is successful in every enterprise he undertakes, not because he is highly talented or cunning, but because a passion for constructive work possesses him, and he accepts no law beyond his own inflexible unruly will. He suffers from no qualms of conscience, which he calls a sickness peculiar to the faint-hearted. In all his words and actions he affirms Gorky's old faith in the efficient individual, self-reliant and devoid of sentimentality. 'If you see a man is strong and capable, help him. But if a man is weak and disinclined to work, spit on him! Wandering pilgrims and parasites complain and groan and go on filling their bellies through other peoples' compassion. You should aid rather the man who in misfortune is a stoic!' When the darker side of Ignat gained control, he would yield to a stormy delirium of the senses. After that storm subsided, he would sink into a submissive, silent penitence and live on bread and water. He beat his first wife because she could not bear him a son. His second wife, a Kazakh woman, Foma's mother, died in childbirth. All his hopes then centred on his only son.

Foma is born the heir to dazzling wealth and splendid opportunity, but his education fails conspicuously to teach him how to use these benefits. His kind aunt fills his mind with remote fairy-tales. His father comes home drunk and tells the child he has a million roubles. 'All is yours.' His guardian, Mayakin, tries to train the boy in the strategy of big business. But the net result is nil. Foma revolts instinctively against the cunning Philistine society which has so carefully prepared an important part for him to play. Yet since he was born and bred within it, knows nothing better, he can find no solid or coherent alternative to fall back upon. Nemesis overtakes him when he becomes aware that he has freed himself from bondage only to sink into a bottomless pit of aimlessness. A fierce joy intoxicated him when he thrashed the Governor's son-in-law at his club, and when he cut the moorings of a raft loaded with people, and watched them drift in terror down the Volga. But these were spasmodic escapades, wild outbursts of a frustrated personality which could not find a path, and rushed into debauch in order to forget the void he felt within himself.

It oppressed him to feel inactive and superfluous, surrounded by busy stevedores, their dirty but smiling faces flushed with work in his employment. Inherited superabundance drove him mad. He could not bear the weight of all that freedom which his millions bought for him so easily. To that extent he proved Mayakin's shrewd prediction to be right. When in the end Foma burst into his dramatic speech, denouncing the merchants collectively and individually, he felt for a moment elated, like a legendary hero who had slain a monster. But then the fire burned out within him, as if he had simultaneously denounced himself and denied his whole *raison d'être*. The indignant merchants promptly took revenge. They made no pretence when they said to him: 'Although we are all Christians, you will get no mercy from us.' And his own guardian shut him up in a lunatic asylum.

Foma, despite his deplorable but human weakness, remains a potent spiritual rebel, because he fell in the unequal fight, without surrendering to his more powerful enemies. Pathetically vague and unstable in positive aims, he was loyal and uncompromising in his aversions. Ilya Lunyov, the hero of Gorky's next novel *Three of Them* (1900), presents a thorough contrast. Starting at the bottom of the bourgeois ladder, instead of at the top, his youthful ambitions and dreams neatly coincide with all the current conventions approved of by a cynical society. He both wants to be, and manages to become, a model shopkeeper, and he commits a murder, which does not even weigh upon his conscience. Yet Gorky evidently implied that even when organized society appears to educate and convert its citizens so thoroughly, it is still dealing with intractable and unpredictable raw material. To achieve this purpose he injects the successful shopkeeper with cumulative boredom and discontent, until in the end he, too, is driven to revolt, runs down a hill and breaks his head against a wall. Though the sequence smacks of artificial melodrama, it reveals the dynamic and consistent movement of Gorky's mind.

To begin with Lunyov is delighted with the pleasant and smooth routine of his own neat haberdashery shop, drinks tea contentedly by the purring *samovar*, thinks with mixed feelings about the seductive police inspector's wife, who had set him up in business, and reads an edifying book in the evening. Then a tattered but carefree casual labourer bewilders him by showing no envy whatsoever for his clean and orderly professional routine. Doubt and disgust assail him and begin to prey upon his mind. At last one day in a frenzy he tears down from his wall the smugly pretty picture, which he used to think so charming, *The Ages of Man*. His last outcry against his fellow shopkeepers is in effect the same as Foma's against the dominant merchants: 'I wanted to find a clean and decent life with you, but, by doing that, I only spoiled myself. . . . A good man can't endure to live with you, he moulders away. You grind good people to death. . . . Yes, I'm angry, but in the midst of you I'm like a weak cat in a dark cellar surrounded by a thousand rats. . . . You are everywhere, you judge, you hire services, you make laws. You're loathsome!'

Despite their sparks of brilliance, their psychological penetration, and vital passages, Gorky's novels and plays of middle-class life are hard to read today. Monotonous, over-loaded with drab detail and irritable argument, they are chaotically pieced together rather than coherently constructed. Too many incidents occur with little or no bearing on the sequence, the philosophic ramblings grow more tedious and repetitive, and the plot always leads to the old *impasse* between aspiring individual misfits and a crushing convention-bound industrial society. The reader is stunned by endless quarrels, floggings, and drunken brawls. Gorky often excused himself by saying that people ought to know about these horrors in order to learn how to uproot them for ever. But Tolstoy, who warmly admired Gorky's early stories, summed up this second literary period with some asperity (in his diary). 'Fame and popularity are most dangerous things. Gorky's novels are worse than his stories, his plays are even worse than his novels, and his appeals to the public are simply repellent. . . . His tremendous heroic emotions ring false.'

Apart from his new pictures of the merchant class, Gorky treated his old enemies, the quasi-intelligentsia, to a new display of angry denunciation in his play, *Dachniki* (1904), and in the

story, *Mujik* (1900). In *Dachniki* one of the more honest characters, Varvara, accuses all the so-called intellectuals of being no
better than camouflaged barbarians, who, while manipulating
high-sounding words about the benefit of mankind, sought
nothing more exalted than a comfortable position for themselves.
'We are not intellectuals, we are really something else. We are
holiday-makers in suburban villas, tourists from abroad. We fuss
around and try to find security for ourselves. But we do nothing
except talk an awful lot.' These people want to hide away from
strife, for no creative purpose either, only to grasp at a cheap little
contentment, enough to eat, comfort and quiet. Rummaging in
their borrowed collection of ideas, coining their fashionable fine
phrases, they crawl like grey phantoms on the fringe of life. Thus
Gorky routed those whom he now called the treacherous *new
barbarians*, self-seeking hypocrites who profitably posed as mis-
sionaries of higher culture, and tried to swindle the long-suffering
public by their clever performing tricks and verbal acrobatics.

But when he comes to the alternative, more genuine and
helpful specimens of the intelligentsia, what comfort does Gorky
manage to provide? We are faced with characters like Nil,
Marya Lvovna, and Vlas, cold, vague, and disembodied types.
Surkov in *Mujik* is little better. Though he honestly tells the
assembled company that they are all bound in the chains of their
own -isms, 'lackeys of their ideas', not even keeping in step with
them, but following passively behind them—he can offer nothing
more constructive in exchange than blind hatred of a nebulous
Philistine.

The architect, Shebyev, goes a step further when he finds fault
with the whole educated class for their dry and doctrinaire preoccupation with superior intellect, for encouraging a breed of
crippled deformities in human shape. To the objection that such
specialization in pure intellect might none the less succeed in
breeding another Immanuel Kant, Shebyev had a ready answer;
Kant was a pathetic and truncated man because he knew nothing
about life beyond his own philosophy; 'Kant and Spinoza were
merely colossal heads, Beethoven an astonishing development of

ears and fingers—but life demands a harmonious human being whose intellect and instincts are fused together.'

Gorky was starting to recoil in some alarm from pursuing to a logical conclusion causes which his own work had unwittingly promoted or stirred up. That ultra-individualist cult, which started as a spiritual protest against mental slavery to a paralysing social hierarchy, defeated its initial purpose, if it later led towards a still more grossly philistine society of self-centred, greedy little minds bowed under a new intellectual Tartar yoke.

VIII

TRAVEL AND EXILE

THE military defeat of Russia by Japan (1904–5) involved Gorky more deeply in struggle against the Government, which had dragged Russia into that disastrous and senseless war. During the 1905 Revolution he was arrested and charged with several political offences. He had written a furious declaration about the events of Bloody Sunday, when the soldiery had fired on an unarmed procession bearing a petition to the Tsar. His faithful friend, the art-loving millionaire, S. Morozov, who had also given money to the Social Democratic Party, immediately provided 10,000 roubles to enable Gorky to be released on bail. The widespread respect which he then inspired abroad, among the educated classes, also stood him in good stead. A chorus of protest arose in the Press of neighbouring countries. The *Berliner Tageblatt* published a vehement letter to the Russian Government, signed by eminent representatives of German literature, science, and art, pleading for his immediate release. Soon afterwards, the nervous Government, anxious to earn esteem by placating foreign opinion, set Gorky free, although it kept him under police supervision. Early in 1906, however, he managed to escape from Russia secretly and reached Berlin.

Thus began the first period of Gorky's European exile. It lasted until February 1913, when he returned to Russia under the formal amnesty granted by the Tsar to political offenders, to celebrate the three hundredth anniversary of the Romanov dynasty. He had gained a valuable breathing space in which to take stock of his own position and also to learn something about foreign countries. Though his literary fame had somewhat waned, the aureole of a revolutionary fighter brought him a new and exhilarating popularity. The Russian Government, more than ever discredited and shaken, needed money urgently, and was trying hard to negotiate a loan from the richer Western countries. Gorky, fresh from a Tsarist prison, an eye-witness of the events of 1905, a renowned champion of the under-dog, appeared to be the best possible ambassador abroad to work for *unofficial* Russia, like Alexander Herzen in the fifties of the previous century.

L. Krassin therefore arranged for him to make a lecture tour in America (April 1906), there to mobilize goodwill and financial support for the Russian opposition parties in their struggle for more political and personal liberty. The tide of events was flowing strongly in his favour. His advent received the widest Press publicity, and he was enthusiastically greeted on his arrival in New York. Unfortunately, he made the blunder of introducing the talented actress who accompanied him, Maria Andreyeva, as his wife, and omitted to mention that his legal wife, from whom he had long been separated, was still alive in Russia.

The Russian Embassy in Washington zealously provided the American Press with ample material to create a resounding public scandal, of which numerous newspapers did not hesitate to take advantage. And Gorky, to his own amazement, found himself changed overnight from a popular idol into a disreputable pariah. Public meetings previously arranged in his honour had to be hurriedly cancelled. He was left standing alone on the New York pavement with his suitcases. One New York hotel after another evicted him, on the ground that guests of such questionable 'morality' as his would drive away their highly respectable family clientèle.

His friends Mr. and Mrs. John Martin made some amends for this outburst of Pecksniffian prudery by giving him and Madame Andreyeva a home for six months in their own house. Some of the metropolitan newspapers treated the affair with dignified reserve, and a few, like the *Independent*, even took Gorky's side. But the social boycott, aimed at by the Russian Embassy, had been achieved. The plan for a triumphal tour of America collapsed completely, and with it vanished the hope of raising much-needed dollars to help the Russian revolutionary movement. Apart from this failure to gauge American mass susceptibilities, Gorky committed a grave tactical blunder. He sent to the American miners, who were then on strike, a congratulatory telegram, and openly took sides with them. Even the most sympathetically disposed Americans were taken aback by such clumsy meddling from a foreign guest. As his shocked supporter, the humorist Mark Twain, expressed it: 'Gorky hits the public in the face with his hat, and then holds it out for contributions. It is more than ludicrous, it is pitiful!'

Gorky's understandable but acutely personal resentment against the American public found further vent in his vitriolic essay, *The City of Mammon*, published in *Appleton's Magazine* in August 1906, and in a letter to his friend, L. Andreyev, where he called America 'the garbage-bin of Europe'. Despite his scanty knowledge of English, and his superficial impressions of New York, he launched into a rhetorical tirade against that city (which, incidentally, he had eloquently praised to journalists on his arrival), calling it an enormous cheerless prison, where the sole freedom known to its millions of inhabitants was that of serving as 'blind tools in the hands of the Yellow Devil—Gold'.

Twenty years later he spoke of this crude generalized abuse with disapproval, and even excused himself by saying: 'I was a Russian rustic then.' [1] But a residue of painful negative impressions remained indelible. Whereas in Russia an overwhelming Asiatic poverty still handicapped and degraded people, here the mental squalor of prosperous Americans appalled him more than the physical squalor of the poor. Indeed, by Russian standards, material poverty had ceased to be a serious problem in America at all. The majority had as much wealth as they knew how to use sensibly, and many had far more than was good for them. 'Already your ordinary workmen have a plethora of material goods,' he said; 'Their souls are stuffed with fatness.' They were unfit to bear the new and unfamiliar burden of abundance.

The failure of Gorky's political and financial mission in

[1] A. Kaun, *M. Gorky*, p. 600.

America revealed his defects as a diplomatic emissary. In compensation, it gave him leisure to write his celebrated novel, *Mother* (first published in 1907). Of all Gorky's works, this has been reprinted the most often, not for its intrinsic merits, which are few, but because it remains the prototype of the modern socially tendentious novel, which (designed to stimulate class warfare) tries to hammer a revolutionary mentality out of a cruel industrial environment. One Soviet critic recently wrote a whole book to prove that this novel laid the foundation stone for the mighty school of socialist realism.[1]

Gorky's own dual intention (rather too blatantly displayed from the start) is, first, to depict how active revolutionary types emerge in frustrated artisans, to whom political revolution, invested with an old revivalist and religious glamour, appears to be the sole alternative to resigned despair—secondly, to create a binding tradition, a sort of revolutionary *old school tie*, a legend of heroic ancestors and loyal colleagues working together for some intelligible common cause. Later Gorky confessed to the Soviet author, F. Gladkov: '*Mother* is a really bad book, written in a state of excitable irritation.'[2]

The *mother* herself, the widow of a brutal factory worker, after a hard life of saintly self-denial, starts to feel drawn towards the revolutionary workmen only when she sees them for the first time in the shape of tormented Christian martyrs (stories of whom were childhood memories for the majority of Russian peasants). By investing these new figures with the old devotional attitude, she can depart from her habitual loyalty to the Orthodox Church without disloyalty to her faith. She substitutes the future paradise on earth for the former dream of personal immortality in heaven. Thus the Orthodox Church, instead of hindering it, unwittingly promotes her emotional transition to revolutionary fervour. In the course of the novel a few characters are psychologically transformed. But among these only the mother is changed with genuine conviction, simply because she feels no need to reason, since her whole being is ruled by love for her only

[1] B. Bursov, *Mat'*, Moscow, 1951.   [2] *Mosty*, No. 1, p. 249, New York, 1959.

F

son. With her no question of *rational* conversion can possibly arise, since all new arguments and doctrines leave her equally unmoved.

The figure of the hero, her son Pavel, now seems painfully forced, rhetorical, and out-of-date. 'We are the first in work,' he complains, 'but the lowest in position. Who worries about us? Who wishes us well? Who treats us like human beings? Nobody.' Of course no contemporary skilled artisan, highly-paid and encouraged everywhere, could honestly echo such sentiments as these. By glorifying the weakest figure in this novel, Soviet critics have made Pavel seem even more artificial than he was. But Gorky deliberately paints the blackest picture of overworked, exasperated factory workers, fierce brutes, like Pavel's father, yet mostly fatalistic slaves of their machines. The mother takes a far more sober view of these contemporary human beings and their superiors, and counsels her impatient son against jumping to premature conclusions. 'Live as you want to, I will not interfere, but I must tell you one thing. Be afraid of people. They all hate one another, they live on greed and envy. The moment you begin to unmask and judge them, they will start also to hate and ruin you.'

Gorky's recurrent figure of the *God-builder* is introduced in the person of the peasant, Rybin, who persuades Pavel that 'God exists in the heart and reason of every man, but not in the Church', and who demands the most practical books designed to rouse the peasants to rebel. The Ukrainian character, Andrei, has more charm and humour than all the other revolutionary workers put together, but he is (if anything specific) a natural anarchist. And so it seems is Pavel, when he breaks his habitual silence and in turn bursts into a tirade against the imprisoning, blood-sucking state. There is not a single exemplary Marxian character among them, and it is hardly surprising that the novel was severely criticized by that pillar of Marxian orthodoxy, Plekhanov, for its glaring failure to translate scientific Socialist teaching into terms of literary art.

The most humanly satisfying relationship achieved in the novel is the friendship formed between the mother and Nicolai Ivano-vich, the urban intellectual, who takes her to live in his house. Gorky writes more warmly about Nicolai, a sympathetic *narod-nik*, than he does about the rather stereotyped factory workers, whom he knew less well from direct experience. Nicolai, a middle-class professional man, did all he could to help the deserving but unfortunate peasants and artisans, and he suffered for his un-selfish actions. The mother looks up to him and respects him.

But his own diagnosis of the social evil with which he grapples is far from flattering to any class, nor does he suggest an easy cure. 'Barbarism is on the increase,' he declares, 'cruelty has become the law of life. Think of it! Some people grow brutal through impunity and succumb to the voluptuous thirst for in-flicting torture—that ugly sickness of slaves who have now received full freedom to vent their servile feelings and bestial habits on others. Some are poisoned by a longing for revenge. And many more, beaten down into a stupor, become both blind and dumb. The people are being ruined, the whole people. . . . And imperceptibly, through all this brutal life, one turns into a beast oneself.'

In October 1906 Gorky settled in Capri, and in the following year he attended the London Conference of the Russian Social Democratic Party, where he first met Lenin. When the Party split into Bolsheviks and Mensheviks, Gorky followed Lenin, whose frank and violent temperament he preferred to the aloof subtlety of the schoolmasterly Plekhanov. Yet Gorky told Lenin, 'I know I am a bad Marxian,' and Lenin admitted to him that he was a brazen opportunist; 'There is nothing holy or sacred about any theories or hypotheses for us; they serve us only as instruments.' [1]

Meanwhile the Western loan, sought by the shaky Russian Government, had been subscribed with the substantial help of French bankers. Gorky seized the occasion to spit in the face of *Fair France* with a fury equal to his earlier denunciation of America in *The Yellow Devil*. He now compared France to an

[1] M. Gorky, *Days with Lenin*, p. 32, Bombay, 1944.

ageing prostitute, whose painted lips had grown pale from thousands of paid kisses. Her best sons of the recent past, Voltaire, Victor Hugo, Flaubert, would, he said, have recoiled in horror from the venal behaviour of contemporary France. He ended his furious pamphlet (*Fair France*, published 1906) 'The blood of the Russian people will once more be shed with the aid of your gold. May this blood suffuse with the red of eternal shame the flabby cheeks of your lying face.'

Like many Russians who admired the West in theory and from a romantic distance, Gorky discovered that Europe and America, seen at close quarters, fell far below his expectations. But although he voiced without restraint his angry disappointment, he did not turn quickly into a rabid xenophobe. In making any broad comparison between the two hemispheres, he had the advantage of knowing Russia intimately.

'We Russians are always attracted by what is dark and evil,' he wrote in 1912. 'In our own obsession with evil we strengthen it around us, hypnotize ourselves. In Europe we look for what most resembles Russia, and finding there filth, swindling, vulgarity, and lies, we are contented—*just like us!* It takes the Russian a long time to find out how Europe *differs* from us, in stable and growing democracy, respect for individuals, capacity for discipline, organization, and productive work in the spiritual sphere. . . . Our craving to pick out the dark and ugly strains in human character shamefully resembles the cunning Philistine desire to drag everybody down to the lowest common level, to obliterate all brighter colours and tones. We dwell preferably on the *failings* of our great men, we point out that Pushkin wrote flattering verse about Nicholas I, that Nekrasov was a gambler, etc.'

In his curious *Letter to a Monarchist* (1912) Gorky claimed that many of these Russian defects were ingredients of the Russian autocratic system, but had lately been enhanced by Russian *patriots*, who now rallied round the monarchy in the name of order and *national character*, yet never attempted to cure their country of such deplorable national characteristics as ignorance, conceit, drunkenness, and foul habits. Moreover these so-called *patriots* were making money for themselves by selling Russian wealth to foreigners, to the German, French, and English industrialists, who were busy opening up the mineral resources of the Urals, the Don Region and Siberia, and the oil of the Caucasus.

Gorky reminded his correspondent that the enlightened novelist, Leskov, had written prophetically: 'In another fifty or a hundred years we shall make ourselves so repugnant to everybody that we shall find ourselves faced with a European coalition against us. Germans will come, new Norsemen, and they will conquer us.' 'Monarchists and patriots, think of these words! It seems that the time which they foresaw is near. Why did the Prussian kings always try to dissuade Alexander III and Nicholas II from introducing radical reforms in Russia. Why does Prussia systematically push the Russian Government towards the Far East, further into Asia? Is it not because it suits them to have a weak and backward neighbour? We shall get involved in Asia for a hundred years of war with China, exhaust our strength . . . in a struggle against that *yellow peril* with which Germans have long since frightened Europeans. And while we are tied hand and foot in Asia, the Germans will take first place in Europe and after-wards put us in good order.'

But Gorky's fears of European political designs to *weaken* Russia in no way detracted from his respect for European achievement, outside the sphere of foreign policy. He drew a clear distinction between his practical hostility to Western industry 'exploiting' untapped Russian wealth, and any mystic opposition to the modern West in its latest industrial or social forms. In a letter to his friend E. Posse (1913), he made his attitude quite explicit: 'One should rather write of what is good in the West, of what may arouse in our citizens envy, emulation, a sense of abuse at home, and similar progressive emotions and sensations. It is necessary that in every letter from abroad our citizens should see above all the advantages of Western life!'

Moreover, Gorky recognized that the old categorical separation of East and West had long ago been broken down in fact. Even barriers of racial heredity set up between East and West were no longer unbridgeable. And that love of constructive action which is (or used to be) so characteristic of the West, must in time also transform the East. 'For now we have seen that the East has partly taken over that astonishingly beautiful, harmonious, and lively union of the whole spiritual work of mankind, which we call Europe, which now includes everything valuable originally created by the East.'

Having trudged through so much of rural Russia, Gorky was familiar with what he called the *Asiatic* strain in Russians, a fleeting excitability, an absence of clearly defined aims or concern for the future, an inclination to indulge in idle day-dreams and cloudy philosophy. They had been dulled by 'the thick heavy blood of the East'. The Russian intelligentsia, he concluded, still formed part and parcel of the semi-Asiatic Russian peasant, both in their defects and in their qualities. Yet it was solely owing to the former that Russians had escaped from remaining sunk in Asiatic immobility and apathy. For the pick of the intelligentsia (let the others go to the Devil!) provided the sole active Western ferment capable of leavening the inert Russian mass. Therefore they could never be *superfluous people*, even when the blind majority treated them as such and gave them no support. 'A Russian writer should be a sacred person. He should *never* live in friendship with the Russian Government—autocratic, constitutional, or republican—our government will be in all three forms equally trashy!' (Letter to L. Andreyev, 1902.)

Gorky here approached his belief in the most useful shape which a Russian revolution ought to take—the alliance of the existing professional class with an *élite* of politically enlightened artisans, against the barbarous anarchic peasantry and the amorphous *Lumpen-proletariat*. Nothing could be more fatal, he urged, than to allow this thinly scattered active minority to dissolve like a handful of salt in the vapid bog of village communities, or unskilled labourers. On the contrary the atavistic instincts of the village masses must and could be conquered and controlled by the superior will and reason of skilled townsmen.

To take the first step in building such an *élite* nucleus of enlightened artisans, was the avowed object of that school for Russian workmen which Gorky founded in Capri. Twenty picked men from factories came there in 1909, to be trained and sent back to Russia as fully-fledged educators of their own class. Gorky engaged the most brilliant Russian specialists to teach them. He told his collaborator, Aleksinsky, that he could count on financial support from a wealthy Russian sympathizer and Maecenas. Bogdanov lectured on political economy, Pokrovsky on political history, Lunacharsky on the history of the labour movement, Aleksinsky on syndicalism and public finance, Gorky himself on the history of Russian literature. Plekhanov never replied to the invitation; Lenin flatly refused; Trotsky promised to come, but never arrived. A popular course with everybody was Lunacharsky's lively one on the history of art, followed by a conducted tour of Rome.

This educational experiment of Gorky's was closely linked with his favourite idea of rescuing modern religion from the stranglehold of established churches, and bringing it down to the conduct of normal human beings. Here he came close to Tolstoy, who at that time was declaring that religion, the most vital thing for man's true welfare, had become, in its perverted forms, the chief source of man's misery. Gorky had expounded this theme in his much-discussed novel, *A Confession* (1908), and more succinctly in his answer to a question about religion sent to him by the French journal *Mercure de France*. There he defined himself as being fundamentally hostile to 'the religions of Moses, Christ, and Mahomet, because they had only succeeded in breeding bitter enmity among men, but strongly in favour of *God-building*, trying to create a new type of human being, the creation of God by man'. So heretical an attempt to fuse personal religion with so-called scientific socialism, and worse still the plan to teach it to impressionable Russian workmen in his own school, brought Gorky into violent conflict with Lenin. Plekhanov also attacked him pontifically in his articles, *About the So-called Religious Quests in Russia*. Lenin wrote rudely that such rubbish was simply 'not worth discussing'. God was merely a complex of ideas produced through the blunt oppression of man by nature. And 'between God-searching and God-building there is about as much difference as between a yellow devil and a blue devil'. Whoever preached the building of a *little God* in man 'would lull to sleep the class struggle'. For Lenin, of course, no crime could possibly be worse than the conquest of class-hatred. He won the day by causing a split among the bewildered students, and officially outlawing Gorky's school from the Bolshevik Party. He had a formal resolution to this effect passed by a conference of the Central Committee. Five of the student artisans then left Capri to join Lenin in Paris, where the remainder joined them at the end of their five months' course in Capri.[1] In the summer of 1910 Lenin paid a diplomatic visit to Gorky in Capri and patched up his personal quarrel with him, which he could well afford to do, after having successfully killed Gorky's school.

[1] See A. Kaun, *Maxim Gorky*, pp. 422–3.

IX

TAKING STOCK OF THE
DEGENERATE

A REVEALING fruit of Gorky's mature reflections on the clever
literary degenerates of his time is the now almost forgotten essay,
which he originally called *From Prometheus to the Hooligan*, and
later published under the more modest title, *The Destruction of
Personality* (1908). It marks a complete revulsion from his early
sympathy for the easy-going vagabond, since he had come to the
conclusion that this human type, pandered to by a period of
mistaken popularity, was breeding a sinister crowd of parasitic
hooligans, creatures devoid of self-respect or social conscience,
incapable of concentrated work, and whose pampered blunted
senses craved for ever cruder and more destructive stimulants.

Looking back on the sweeping social changes of the past
decades, Gorky called attention to an acute disharmony between
the growth of personal moral character and the routine occupational demands imposed on it by modern industrial technique, a
conflict which had resulted almost everywhere in debilitating
nervous strain, accompanied by degeneracy. Mechanical urban
organization and methods, plus their by-product, the hooligan,
spreading rapidly and relentlessly into every sphere and every
class, were hand in hand disintegrating human personality. He
pointed out that neurasthenia, mental disease, and criminal out-
breaks had spread most markedly, *not* among primitive or
poverty-stricken people, but in materially prosperous families,
especially in America and Russia, historically younger countries,
but subject to the most rapid recent industrial advance. At the
same time, both in Russia and throughout the Western world, the
children and grandchildren of the strong, vital, 'successful' men

of the mid-nineteenth century had grown progressively weaker and shallower.

The time had now come when these decrepit descendants of robust ancestors, suddenly frightened for their own survival, rallied against surrender to the course of further social change. They justified their resistance by claiming that they must stand firm to defend their inherited culture against the inroads of *new Huns*. A false and hypocritical claim, Gorky contended, because hardly an atom of genuine culture could still be found in their own empty and disordered minds. They themselves stood for nothing worth preserving. And they blankly ignored the true and timeless inheritance of past centuries which, if anywhere, lay neglected and buried in tomb-like art museums and libraries, where sleepy indifferent watchmen stood on guard over a cemetery of moribund values.

On the whole, intellectual movements of the last two decades had passively mirrored this gradual social self-destruction, or corruptly pandered to it. Writers no longer made any bold attempt to go beyond it, to guide, inspire, or enlighten people, as they had done before. They set no clear example and maintained no firm ideals. For the average writer of this sick and nervous period had altogether lost that integrity and imaginative fire, sacred to the preceding generation. He had turned into a self-centred professional man of letters, a paid hireling, anxious above all to please his clients, and terrified of growing unpopular or going out of fashion. His style became thinner, sharper, and more colourless, his tone sounded colder. Independent thought, for him, had lost its wings, and sunk into the dust of everyday life, where it fell apart in sombre fragments. Calm courage had degenerated into vulgar impudence, defence of justice into calculating self-advertisement, righteous indignation into petty spite. The soul of the imaginative writer had ceased to be an Aeolian harp, vibrating in response to every new and pure impression of the life around him. He could more easily play the part of an ingratiating jester, a chronicler of the trivial, or a lurid scandal-monger, and carefully studied how he could most profitably

shock or amuse the reading public, when it grew tired or
bored.

The psychology of the older Russian men of letters, whatever
their political orientation, had always reached depths and heights
transcending the limits of any social doctrines or fashions promoted by their age. Men like Tolstoy and Turgenev had proved
themselves to be, and still remained, spiritual guides or prophets
in their own right. But such men, who *used* to be looked up to as
educators and leaders of the people, had gradually been replaced
by irresponsible Bohemians, by cynical frequenters of the public-
house and the lower music-hall. They arranged obscene pictures
in pretty frames, exalted prostitution as *self-realization*, and
attractively disguised neglect of duty as a sacred freedom of
choice. A nadir of spiritual bankruptcy had been reached in
Artsybashev's novel, *Sanin*, a best-seller, which plainly reduced
the Russian hero to the level of 'a lustful he-goat dressed in
trousers'. This work had swept the public off its feet, thus
proving that pornography now paid the highest dividends, and
had become the surest key to modern literary success.

In considering Gorky's diatribe and its applicability, we
should remember that the virtual abolition in 1905 of the hitherto
severe Russian censorship had proved a bitter disappointment.
True, it allowed for the first time in Russian history the publication of separate political journals, including Marxian ones, and
thus at last absolved writers of *belles lettres* from their perfunctory concentration on political and social problems. Many
sanguine people felt convinced that Russian literature, so long
polluted by the muddy political stream, would take on a new
lease of life through this long-sought emancipation from Government bondage and political controversy. But they were proved
to be mistaken. The most striking result of the relaxed censorship
was, not an outburst of fresh creative talent, but a steadily mounting flow of cheaply sensational, trivial, or pornographic fiction,
which made easy money for its authors and publishers, but slowly
poisoned public taste and feeling.

These decadent best-sellers have long since been consigned to the oblivion which they deserve. But, while they lasted, they indirectly served the Revolutionary cause by helping the morale of society to sink more rapidly. In contrasting their vulgar squalor with the grandeur and pathos of their predecessors, Gorky was not indulging in such a crude over-generalized statement as any reader, unfamiliar with the literary climate of the period, might think. Gorky plainly condemned the present by the higher spiritual standards of the past (which he did not confuse with its achievements). He felt no need to hunt for any new criterion, because he never accepted the fashionable historical opinion, that every separate age brought its own peculiar moral and aesthetic standards, and therefore that the march of history could justify anything apparently new, however false and vile. He would not allow the glow of past glory on ugly modern sores, to be advertised as the blushes of promising youth.

In this attempt to face the plain facts of mental degeneration honestly, Gorky had a lot in common with his contemporary Chekhov. Both recognized that the old intellectual class, *de guerre lasse*, grown weak and time-serving, was giving up the hard exacting struggle, and selling its services, either to the government or to plain commercial interests. Pure imaginative literature in the older sense, expressing some philosophic faith or strong spiritual talent, was coming to an end. It involved commercial publishers in too much financial risk, and the equally commercial-minded government saw no political need for it. The former found it easier and safer to coarsely entertain or pleasantly horrify the public, while the latter wanted an endlessly repeated string of edifying civic platitudes, supported by new statistics. The result encouraged deadly mediocrity or bred artistic lunacy.

In the end, the gradually paralysed writer ceased to care, so long as he could sell his wares and make a living. Gorky dimly recognized this last surrender, but his over-emphatic temperament never enabled him to describe it so lucidly as Chekhov did in the figure of his tipsy school-teacher, who delivered the following symbolic speech to the portrait of the Roman philosopher, Seneca: 'You knew how to preach patience, you were wise and clear-sighted; but you could not in your time foresee that, eighteen centuries after your death, people would approach the art of life with empty hearts, and would be far more *indifferent* than you ever intended them to be, when you pleaded for patience. . . . For now people have grown equally indifferent to good and evil, and, being drained of spiritual strength, surrender easily to the blows of fate, submit to daily slavery without a struggle and without any sense of shame. . . . I am like that, Seneca, and so are many.'

Despite his undeniably low opinion of the new literary generation as a whole, Gorky took a friendly interest in the works of any gifted young writers he could find, and had published many of them in his journal, *Jizn*. But he always remained an exacting critic. Vague composition, clumsy situations, limp inexact language, all provoked in him stern judgements. Though he was always hopefully on the look-out for fresh 'proletarian' talent, he never encouraged young writers through inverted class-prejudice, merely because they had the fashionable merit of being dock-labourers or beggars, and he stood no nonsense from pretentious self-advertising upstarts.

The mentally diseased, chaotic, or coldly abstract *genre*, which came to the fore in late nineteenth-century art, he met with clear and undiluted hostility, whether it appeared in Vrubel's more deformed paintings, Remizov's long-winded pathological novels, or in Andreyev's dreary stilted plays. For that reason he rejected Remizov's story, *The Pond*, when it was proposed for publication in *Znanie*. Already in 1896, when reviewing the All-Russian Exhibition at Nijni Novgorod for the *Samara Gazette*, he had inveighed against the so-called modernist intellectual movements corrupting both visual and verbal arts. 'We have quite enough in life itself of things shadowy, dim, distorted, and depressing, without encouraging the fabrications of this new firm of Vrubel, Balmont, Gippius, etc. Life demands more light and clarity, but has no need for obscure repulsive paintings or nervously morbid verse, devoid of all benefit to human beings and infinitely removed from genuine art.'

X

UNDERSTANDING HIS CREATIVE CONTEMPORARIES

During his stay in Capri, Gorky found himself inundated with appeals for help and advice from a motley crowd of newly literate Russian writers. He took them all seriously—often more so than they deserved—and would spend many hours covering the manuscripts, which they sent him, with marks, comments and corrections, in red, blue, and green pencil. Yet most of these self-taught aspirants failed to pass his own exacting test of talent. No music of language, no mastery of precise description, or fluidity of thought, Gorky frequently complained. At times he could be brutally frank. 'Your language is impossible,' he wrote to one correspondent, 'firstly, you never feel the rhythm of a sentence and pay no attention to its sound; then, despite your verbal eloquence, your vocabulary is dim, poverty-stricken, and devoid of imagery. Once you employ the verb "to be" eight times in a single page. Unpardonable!'

But Gorky noted in their favour that some of these artisans regarded their tentative literary efforts with a touching modesty, unknown to more smugly self-satisfied candidates of the lower middle class. He quoted approvingly a letter written to him by a naïve and clumsy workman (*Self-Taught Writers*, 1911): 'If you find I have no ability, I will drop writing altogether and seek a more suitable work. Please be merciless. Do not hesitate to tell me the truth, however sad for me. I know that an author's vocation is a sacred one!'

Gorky repeatedly advised beginners, both before and after the Revolution, to study thoroughly the Russian classics. 'Read Pushkin, Turgenev, and Chekhov, who are all connoisseurs of plastic language.' F. Gladkov, who later became a successful Soviet novelist, admitted that his correspondence with Gorky had immense educational significance for him. The ex-sailor, Novikov-Priboi, who wrote a celebrated novel about the Russo-Japanese War, was invited by Gorky to visit him in Capri, and then stayed there for a whole year. Of course these were both exceptional men of humble origin, who thrust themselves upwards by their vital, forceful talent, as Gorky had done before. He liked to think that many other buried souls would rise from the darker depths as soon as they got their chance.

But it is a mistake to claim that the October Revolution upset Gorky's early standards or biased his literary judgement in favour of the plebeian. He regretted the continued but undeniable rarity of talent in any and every social class. When, after he had retired to Sorrento in 1921, the editor of a popular magazine implored him to treat more leniently the hundreds of manuscripts now sent to him by Russian artisans and peasants, he replied indignantly: 'We must not divert a workman from his regular trade for the sake of any cheap popular success in writing. It is a shame and a crime thus to breed mental mediocrity among the people; it is wrong to encourage their conceit.' In 1911 Stanislavsky went to Capri to visit Gorky, and they discussed theatrical experiments involving much closer collaboration between actors, producer, and author—an addition to Stanislavsky's famous *method*.

After his return to Russia from Italy in 1914, and during the first World War, Gorky edited a monthly journal called *Letopis.* Infinitely more important, this period saw the beginning of that brilliant autobiographical series, on which his lasting literary reputation has come largely to depend. During that time Gorky abandoned his long-winded and scrappy topical novels. By transforming his work into a pure retrospective chronicle, he managed to conquer his less fruitful introspective habits. The quests of disgruntled misfits who never find anything definite or firm, the tedious, disjointed argument, so burdensome in his novels, died away. The most arresting feature common to all these autobiographical books is their deliberate self-effacement. Hardly less remarkable (for Gorky) is their calm objectivity and vivid economy of phrase. Unique in their absence of self-absorption, they excel in authentic pictures of his Russian environment and the many strange people he had met in it.

Childhood (1913), followed by *Among People* (1915), and *My Universities* (1923), we have already considered in their relation to Gorky's early life and the stories which he wrote about his wanderings. *Recollections* (1923) broke into a new medium. It left the sphere of narrative and gave a close-up view of some of his most eminent contemporaries, Karonin, Tolstoy, Chekhov, Kotsyubinsky, and Andreyev. Gorky's judgement of all these complex individuals is refreshingly clear-sighted and free from prejudice. It swept aside the muddled fashionable labels of the day, and in a few pages, packed with acute observation, threw more revealing light on their subjects than some literary historians have managed to convey in volumes of intricate analysis.

Gorky started to *see through* Tolstoy simply by observing that Tolstoy at close quarters was totally unlike the image of himself which he had recently projected upon the outside world. He felt, though he may not properly have understood, secrets which Tolstoy preferred to hide from everybody. That partly explains why their personal relations remained ambiguous and uneasy, and why Tolstoy said about him: 'Gorky has the mind of a spy'. He told Chekhov: 'Gorky has the nose of a duck. Only unhappy and unkind men have noses like that.' Gorky knew, from the tone underlying Tolstoy's ready flow of words, that there was still much about which he preferred to remain silent. He noted that Tolstoy talked about his favourite Buddhism in a sentimental tone, and about Christ 'coldly and wearily', without a spark of feeling or enthusiasm in his voice. He was impressed by Countess Tolstoy's courage in opposing her husband, and by her devotion to her children.

He recognized how Tolstoy had become aware that his latest evangelical preaching lacked power to convince people, how he already regarded his cranky Tolstoyan disciples with a scarcely veiled aversion, and how he longed to suffer some kind of

martyrdom, imprisonment, or banishment, in order to make his
ethical ideas more irresistible, and thus bring worthier followers
to respect them.

Moreover, apart from a persistent spiritual ambition to influence people and events, Gorky saw a pathetic, tired old man
who felt condemned to play the part which was expected of him,
a prisoner of his self-created legend, who could not force himself
to disappoint his exacting public. Tolstoy even confessed to
Gorky in an unguarded moment: 'I never lived for myself; I lived
too much for show, for *other* people.' The demands of too many
people had distracted him from the essential quest.

Thus the legend of the repentant sinner and voluptuary, the
saintly convert, surrounded by disciples or admirers, the rational
evangelist who brought the Gospels up to date, the creator of his
country's latest social conscience, faded in front of Gorky's
penetrating gaze. A far more enigmatic figure took its place, a
pagan old magician, amazing and brilliant even in his glaring
contradictions, an utterly lonely pilgrim travelling through
deserts of thought in search of some oasis which he never found,
and oppressed by strange forebodings of which he was afraid to
speak.

'I do not know,' Gorky concluded, 'whether I loved him, but
does it really matter, love or hatred? He always aroused in me
sensations which were enormous, fantastic; even my hostile
feelings were of a kind, not to depress, but rather to expand the
soul, to make it more sensitive and capacious. . . .' Tolstoy had
said to him: 'A non-believer cannot love. He will have affairs with
one woman after another. Such men have vagabond hearts and
their lives are vain. But you were born a believer, and it is useless
to try to violate yourself. . . . You speak about beauty. What is
it? The highest and most perfect is God. . . . People who love
are talented.' 'And I,' Gorky continued, 'though not believing in
God, look at him very carefully, almost timidly, look and think:
that man is God-like!'

About his closer friend, Andreyev, Gorky wrote with surprising sympathy, despite the fact that he flatly disagreed with

G

him. He liked him entirely against his rational judgement, as a gifted and picturesque degenerate, who might have been saved, despite his drunken orgies, his craze for paradox, for eccentric devilish coloured waistcoats and absurd yellow boots. 'I never,' Gorky explained, 'gave theories or opinions any deciding role in my relations with other people.' Andreyev none the less provided an object-lesson in that relentless disintegration of personality which Gorky had described in his essay of that name.

He was always ready to justify his instinctive urge for self-destruction. He used to say: 'Gifted Russians must go to the brothel, otherwise the critics will never admit how talented they are! Better to be a consummate blackguard than a righteous man who can't drag himself up to the height of saintliness.' Thus Andreyev cast off with a flourish all those extraneous social obligations, perpetually thrust upon Russian writers, to be ideal liberals, socialists, revolutionaries, or reactionaries—anything but their natural unruly selves! Unfortunately he found nothing more solid to fall back upon than a metaphysical morass, tried to intoxicate himself with stimulating words instead of with alcohol, and then began to recognize that even his flow of language was ossifying and drying up.

His tenuous friendship with Gorky was finally broken by the Revolution. He then accused Gorky of having lived so long abroad that he had been corrupted by non-Russian methods of violent and bloody struggle. He interested Gorky finally as a specimen of *period pathology*, who had sunk too low to be cured, and indeed never wanted to be cured, but gloried in worshipping himself as the perfect pearl which could grow only in a thoroughly infected shell. Gorky had told him reprovingly: '*I* do not want to poison other people with the shameful vision of all my own wounds and sores.' But that very sentence aptly defined the perverse *genre* of literary art in which Andreyev had excelled, and for which Gorky gave him due credit.

To Chekhov, alone among his literary contemporaries, Gorky felt drawn both by deep respect and intimate personal sympathy.

He derived unfailing solace and support from Chekhov's faith in those few *dependable* members of the Russian intelligentsia who still thought honestly, felt strongly, and knew how to work hard. He even solicited and benefited by Chekhov's friendly criticism of his own literary defects. 'He had the art of showing up and everywhere driving away *banality*. . . . Chekhov infected people with a desire to be simpler and more genuine. In his presence people shed that motley finery of bookish phrases, smart words, and all the other cheap tricks with which a Russian, trying to figure as a European, adorns himself, like a savage with shells and fishes' teeth.'

Gorky also happily singled out Chekhov's attitude to useful contemporary work as being identical to his own. Through all those inconsequent characters in his plays, who talk so charmingly about the supreme importance of useful and regular work—and themselves remain perfect idlers—or dream about how divinely beautiful life will become three hundred years later—but fail to notice that, through their own slovenly neglect, people and things are rapidly crumbling to ruin all around them—he felt that Chekhov intended to convince his audience how deeply he believed that self-reliant, sensible, and industrious people (the exact reverse of his own feckless, moody, and lazy characters) must form the only possible foundation for any future human culture. He noticed in Yalta how Chekhov loved to build, to plant his garden with fruit trees and shrubs, to make his small property grow more delightful.

Gorky, rightly or wrongly, interpreted Chekhov's elusive ideals as if they were his own. He fully endorsed his detailed diagnosis of the main Russian ills. And he generously admitted that Chekhov's gentle, crystalline sketches left a stronger, more lasting after-taste on the reader than many of his own turgid, angry stories. He drew attention to the deep note of reproach which he detected underneath the quiet subtle humour and exquisite finesse of Chekhov's language. He even admired in him a sharply sceptical irony which he refrained from admitting in himself, perhaps for fear that it might damage his *alter ego*, and detract from his hard-earned public reputation as a belligerent social optimist.

Chekhov's remarks to him, which he scrupulously recorded, about the tragi-comic inconsequence peculiar to Russian professional men, were pronounced in a whimsical manner, which Gorky could not, or dared not, emulate, but which he evidently endorsed: 'A Russian is like a sieve; nothing stays long inside him. An architect, having built a couple of decent houses, sits down one day to play cards, and goes on playing cards for the rest of his life. A doctor, as soon as he has got a practice, loses all interest in medicine, reads nothing except the *Medical Journal*, and at the age of forty seriously believes that all diseases have their origin in catarrh. I have never met a single civil servant who has given one thought to the sense of his work. . . . An actor, after having played two or three parts tolerably, no longer troubles to learn his parts at all, puts on a silk hat, and calls himself a genius. Russia is full of such insatiable but lazy people. . . . They marry in order to get their houses looked after, and then take mistresses in order to gain prestige in society. Their psychology is that of a dog.'

'And in front of that dreary grey crowd,' Gorky summed up, 'there passed a great, wise, and observant man.' Never did he express such whole-hearted sympathy with another writer's outlook on that society which provided such abundant but exasperating raw material for them both. Nor did he ever write so warmly about any other human being. As his intimate letters prove, he felt at ease with Chekhov, who understood him without superfluous words, without an atom of professional jealousy, and poured balm upon his many unhealed wounds.

XI

GORKY AND THE REVOLUTION

PROFITING from the political amnesty granted by Nicolas II, Gorky had returned to Russia early in 1914. He refused to appear at any public manifestations arranged in his honour, and shortly after his arrival he retired to a villa in Finland. In 1915 he started to edit a monthly review called *Letopis*, broadly pacifist and international in tone. This activity conclusively branded him as defeatist, if not pro-German, in the eyes of Russian patriots during the first World War. Both the Marxian, Plekhanov, and the anarchist, Kropotkin, despite their hatred of the Tsarist regime, had pronounced unequivocally in favour of Russian national defence against the military aggression of the German Empire. Thus Gorky began to represent a profoundly unpopular and suspect minority. But his pacifist fixation betrayed considerable constraint, for it went against the grain both of his own latent national pride and his characteristic spirit of revolt.

It is desirable to correct some still current misconceptions about Gorky's real attitude to the February and October Revolutions (1917). When the first Revolution overthrew the monarchy, he became acutely troubled by the appalling prospect of unbridled national anarchy. In his revived journal, *New Life* (*Novaya Jizn*), he concentrated on the need for government intervention to save Russian culture from being ruined beyond repair by public indifference to the past, and by giving free rein to private vandals. He tried to avoid taking sides on topical issues, which irritated and distracted him. Only when the latest political upheavals and plans threatened to engulf all else, including his own work, he had to strike out vehemently. He still regarded the Bolsheviks as one among several parties and factions sincerely

aiming at an improved democratic state. Therefore in October
1917 he wrote a strong prophetic editorial (*One must not be
silent*) in *New Life*, warning against the untold miseries which
would be unleashed by a premature *coup d'état*! [1]

'Ever more persistent rumours are spreading to the effect that
on October 20th a Bolshevik rising may take place. . . . All the
dark instincts of the crowd, irritated by the social disorder, falsehood, and filth, brought out by political agitation, will flare up
and give vent to poisonous malice, hatred, and vengeance. People
will start to murder one another, through sheer inability to overcome their own bestial stupidity. . . . The unorganized crowd
will creep out into the streets, hardly understanding what it
wants, while under its cover, adventurers, thieves, and professional assassins will set out to create the *history of the Russian
Revolution*. . . . In brief, there will be another bloody and senseless slaughter, such as we have already witnessed, and which has
undermined through our country the moral importance of the
Revolution and shaken its cultural meaning.' Some of the leading
Bolsheviks fully agreed with Gorky in objecting to the Party
taking initiative for any armed rising in the immediate future.
Kamenev published a letter to that effect in *New Life*, speaking for himself, Zinoviev, and a number of other influential
'comrades'. But the confirmed Leninists poured scorn on
New Life, and the Bolshevik, *Noviy Put'*, already wrote of
it sardonically: 'The revolution neither buries nor pities its
corpses.'

Meanwhile Lenin and Trotsky carefully plotted and planned
their military *coup d'état*, so that even the notoriously loyal
Cossack regiments refused to obey Kerensky's orders. But as
soon as the October Revolution had effectively overthrown and
replaced the Kerensky Government, Gorky attacked the now
triumphant Bolsheviks with still more impassioned vehemence.
The article he published in *New Life* on November 7th (O.S.)
spared them nothing. Lenin, Trotsky, and their supporters, have

[1] M. Gorky, *Revolyutsia i Kultura, Statyi za 1917*, p. 55, Berlin, 1920. (Not re-
published in the Soviet edition of Gorky's collected works.)

already been poisoned by the corruptive virus of power, which is evident from their disgraceful treatment of freedom of speech and person, and of all those rights for which democracy has struggled. . . . Along this road Lenin and his henchmen deem it right to commit every crime, such as the slaughter near Petrograd, the bombardment of Moscow, the abolition of free speech, senseless arrests—exactly the same abominations formerly perpetrated by Plehve and Stolypin. To be sure, Stolypin and Plehve acted against democracy, against all that was alive and decent in Russia, whereas Lenin is followed, for the time being, by a fairly important section of the workmen. But I am convinced that the workmen's good sense, their understanding of their historical tasks, will soon open their eyes to the unattainability of Lenin's promises, to the depths of his madness, to his *Nechayev–Bakunin* brand of anarchy. . . . The workmen must understand that, with their skins and blood, Lenin is performing an experiment . . . that there are no miracles in ordinary life, that they must expect hunger, complete dislocation of industry, ruin of transport, prolonged bloody anarchy—and in its wake a no less bloody and gloomy reaction. That is where the people are being led by its present leader. We must recognize that Lenin is not an omnipotent magician, but a cold-blooded trickster, who spares neither the honour nor the lives of the proletariat.'

On November 10th (O.S.) Gorky labelled Lenin's followers 'Napoleons of socialism', and despite his former friendship with Lenin, did not shrink from denouncing him personally, while giving him his due. 'Lenin is, of course, a man of exceptional force. . . . He has all the qualities of a leader, including the indispensable amoral quality and an aristocratic merciless attitude to the lives of common people. . . . Life in its real complexity is unknown to Lenin. He does not know the masses of the people. He has never lived among them. Only from books he learned how to raise this mass on to its haunches, and how most effectively to rouse its instincts to a fury. . . . He is working like a chemist in his laboratory—with this difference—that the chemist employs dead matter to gain results valuable for life, whereas Lenin works on living material and is leading the revolution to disaster.' (*New Life*.)

In further articles following in this series, Gorky accused demagogues like Zinoviev, of craftily debauching honest artisans, inflaming their lowest instincts, pushing the genuine workers' friends aside into the tragic predicament of becoming strangers and suspects to their own people. He pointed out that, in the factories, envious unskilled labourers were being incited by Bolshevik agitators to assert that highly qualified carpenters, turners, founders, etc., were merely *bourgeois traitors*. He complained that the Bolshevik journal, *Pravda*, employed contemptible hireling writers to rouse the rabble against skilled and valuable educated people, in the name of *class-warfare*. No wonder that any self-respecting professional man would rather *starve* than accept to work for a government which now printed the threat to establish 'a special council of Red Sailors in order to murder a hundred thousand *bourgeois* for every single one of its own comrades, and suchlike balderdash!'

Pravda retaliated against these furious attacks by accusing Gorky of having deserted to the enemies of 'revolutionary democracy', and by inquiring sarcastically whether he would be a welcome guest at the future *bright festival of peoples*, when former involuntary enemies would merge at last in one brotherly embrace! Gorky evaded falling into this rhetorical trap and replied in his own paper: 'It goes without saying that neither the author of the article, nor I, will live to see that *bright festival*. It is too remote, and many decades of stubborn workaday labour will be required to make it possible. But at a festival where the despotism of the semi-literate mass will celebrate its vulgar victory, and human personality as before will be in chains, I shall have nothing to do, and for me that will be no festival at all!' (*New Life*, 19 November (O.S.) 1917.)

Since *New Life* could no longer steer clear of the political events which were swamping Russia, it went on battling hard against those which it deemed calamitous. It described the Brest-Litovsk Treaty with Germany as 'a shameful betrayal of the

country and the revolution' by 'a band of adventurers'. In more
measured terms it condemned the Soviet proposal to ban the
Kadet Party (Constitutional Democrats) from the Constituent
Assembly. 'Apart from the fact that an appreciable part of the
population *want* the Kadets to represent their opinions and desires
—I affirm that in this Party are some of the most cultured people
in the country, the most able in all spheres of mental work! . . .
A firm enemy can educate his opponent!' Inevitably *New Life*
started to be persecuted. From time to time, the typesetters,
incited by agitators, refused to print outspoken articles, so that
the paper appeared with blank sheets or even had to skip an issue.
But such an unequal struggle could hardly continue. It is rather
surprising that Lenin put up with it for so long. Towards the end
of 1918 he decided to suppress *New Life*, so that Gorky found
himself stranded without an independent organ.

The suppression of *New Life* may have been a blessing in
disguise. It rescued Gorky from vainly trying to check or reform
the triumphant Bolsheviks by means of writing angry newspaper
articles about them. He could at last devote his wasted energy to
a more practicable and congenial task—to rescue Russian art
treasures from common thieves and vandals, and brilliant
Russian scientists, authors, and artists, from unemployment,
misery, or sheer starvation. During the chaotic period between
1918 and 1920 many of these unfortunate people owed their
survival to his immense and absolutely disinterested efforts. Apart
from those who were killed, the Revolution inflicted cold, hunger,
arbitrary arrest, deprivation of work, and all kinds of petty
humiliation. In the name of egalitarianism, it was quite normal for
professional people to be suddenly evicted from their homes and
offices, and forced to clean the streets. In the Academy of Sciences,
every employee, whether an aged scientist or a burly porter,
received orders one winter to take turns in guarding for six hours
the firewood stacked along the pavement. Gorky would often
intervene to provide a little food for starving writers who had
attacked him viciously before the Revolution. On one occasion
he obtained (albeit too late) an order signed by Lenin to stop four

Grand Dukes from being shot by order of the Petrograd *Cheka*. Only one of them (the Grand Duke Gabriel) was saved from the firing squad. He spared neither his own health nor his dangerously *unrevolutionary* reputation with the ruling party. He showed astonishing magnanimity, courage, and initiative. As the writer, V. Shklovsky, observed: 'An Academician is for Gorky a fine piece of porcelain with a rare mark. And he is ready to be broken to save that porcelain.' [1]

He managed to secure the Government's support to found a Commission for improving the Living Conditions of Scholars, a *Writer's Home*, a *Home of the Arts*, a Commission to preserve historic monuments, and above all, measures to facilitate food rations and medical aid for 'mental workers'. His project, *World Literature*, provided employment for hundreds of distressed writers in translating the most important literary classics of many foreign countries into the Russian language. Many of these translations, although completed, were never published, because the Government found later that it needed all its scanty paper supplies for more urgent utilitarian publications. And some disgruntled writers complained that they were, in fact, only paid enough to starve slowly. Others were more grateful. The author, Vsevolod Ivanov, recorded that two letters which he received from Gorky during those grim years were 'like two wings which protected me and drew me away from death'.

It was high time to start saving magnificent buildings and irreplaceable art-treasures from malicious damage and gross neglect. Hordes of peasants, sacking country houses, hacked pianos to pieces with their axes, tore up priceless paintings, made bonfires of beautiful furniture and fine books. In towns equally destructive looting took place, especially after crowds had broken into wine-cellars and drunk their fill. Gorky pointed to the ominous fact that the wanton desecration of ancient monasteries and churches aroused no sign of protest whatsoever from fickle multitudes, who only yesterday had reverently prostrated themselves and prayed in those same miracle-working places.

[1] V. Shklovsky, *Udachi i Porazhenia*, Moscow, 1926.

In 1919, during a Peasant Congress in Petrograd, some hundreds of them were lodged in the Winter Palace. Although the palace plumbing was in good order, the new lodgers deliberately befouled for lavatory use precious porcelain vases and ornaments. 'Two revolutions and a war have supplied me with hundreds of cases which reveal this lurking, vindictive tendency in people to smash, mutilate, ridicule, and defame beautiful things. It must not be thought that I pick out the conduct of these villagers because of my sceptical attitude towards the peasants. That is not so. I know some groups of intellectuals who suffer from exactly the same morbid craving to defile whatever is beautiful. . . . That malicious desire is identical with the odious tendency to vilify any exceptional human being.' [1]

Gorky's Commission to preserve fine buildings and art treasures in Russia had therefore to fight hard, because the authorities then paid scanty attention to things connected with the past. But many works of art, confiscated from private owners by the Soviet Government, were being sold in Berlin to raise sorely needed foreign exchange. Gorky's friend, the actress, Marya Andreyeva, played an active part in these transactions, and he himself started to collect rare books, pieces of Chinese carved jade, and Buddhist sculpture. Evidently pangs of conscience troubled him, for many objects came from the pillage of private houses, or had been sold at low prices by cultured people fallen into desperate poverty. He gave his books away most readily, and his works of art he later handed over to the Russian Museum in Petrograd.

He had earlier succeeded in persuading the Party's Executive Committee to circulate the text of an appeal to the Russian public. Even if such appeals fell on deaf ears at first, he felt that they must be tried out and repeated. This one is characteristic of those ardently conservative admonitions, which Gorky now perseveringly impressed upon his Soviet audiences. 'Citizens,' he urged, 'guard your own inheritance. Guard the palaces, for they will become palaces of your national art. Guard the pictures,

[1] M. Gorky, *Days with Lenin*, p. 25, Bombay, 1944.

statues, and buildings, for these are the embodiment of your own spiritual power, and that of your ancestors. Art consists of those fine things which gifted human beings have created, even under the oppression of despotism, and which testify to the power and beauty of the human mind. . . . Remember that this is the soil from which your new national art must grow!'

Though Gorky cursed the Bolsheviks in their hour of triumph, he rallied to them during the Civil War at a moment when their fortunes had fallen to their lowest ebb. His reconciliation with Lenin started in 1919, immediately after the latter had been wounded by the Social Revolutionary, who attempted to assassinate him.

It is therefore false to assert, as some of his enemies have done, that Gorky bowed to the Bolsheviks, merely because they stayed in power. Undoubtedly the intervention of the Western allies in the Russian Civil War contributed to his change of heart, for it roused his anger against what he termed the *wicked hypocrisy* of Western Governments. The appeal which he published in 1919, *Follow Us*, lashed out in particular against the American President Wilson 'who only yesterday was the eloquent champion of peoples' autonomy and rights of democracy, and is now equipping a powerful army to restore order in revolutionary Russia, where the people have already exercised their lawful right to take power into their own hands.'

Pravda seized this opportunity to announce with loud applause that the Bolsheviks had won a substantial new victory; they had reconquered Maxim Gorky. He had said: 'Comrades, let us forget the past', and both he and they were happy to forget it. So the prodigal son returned home and festive rejoicing followed. This official reconciliation immensely facilitated Gorky's dealings with the Soviet authorities, who promptly used him to raise their own prestige. For foreign consumption, his name and reputation advertised the progress of humane culture in the blood-bath of the nascent socialist state. And at home he served as a new rallying point to reconcile many dissidents still openly in conflict with the Soviet regime.

He received a high-sounding post in the Ministry of Public Instruction, and placed himself at the disposal of the Government to figure on ceremonial occasions, especially in the reception of foreign delegates, and of influential writers, such as H. G. Wells and Romain Rolland. During the 1921 famine Gorky's personal appeals played a decisive part in promoting the generous aid poured into Russia by American philanthropic societies, which saved millions of people from starving to death. The scandal and enmity which Gorky had aroused in America in 1906, his virulent *City of Mammon* and *Kingdom of Boredom*, were now forgotten or discounted by indulgent American citizens.

Many Russians, chiefly *émigrés*, hurled abuse at Gorky, and regarded his *conversion* as nothing but an act of treachery for the sake of self-advancement. His former friend and colleague on *Znanie*, the socialist writer, Chirikov, called him a chameleon, changing his colour according to the political wind and weather, deplored his humiliating repentance and 'the odious servility of his speeches'.[1] He complained that Gorky sold for several million roubles to the Soviet Government the rights to publish a new edition of his collected works (the same rights which he had sold once before to the publisher of *Niva*, Marx) and was now busy exhorting the whole educated class to sell its soul to the sinister Soviet power, just as he had done himself.

It is undeniable that Gorky, after his spell of public denunciation of the Bolsheviks, turned with surprising alacrity to the opposite extreme, by serving as their principal publicity officer. But Chirikov admits no extenuating circumstances, or sober consideration of the barren alternatives facing Gorky. Forced to choose between two evils, Gorky chose what seemed to him the lesser one. Without some Government support, his valuable non-political work in Russia would have had to be abandoned, and the Government gave him a much freer hand than any other man, with a less important international standing, would ever have received. The price he had to pay did not at first seem unduly high for what he was getting in return. As for the publication of his

[1] E. Chirikov, *Smerdyakov Russkoi Revolutsiy*, Sofia, 1921.

works, Gorky can hardly be blamed for making a new business arrangement with the state, since his former private publishers had vanished from the scene.

In 1921, worn out by overwork, vexation, and failing health, Gorky left Russia, spent a short time in a German sanatorium, and then travelled to Sorrento, where he settled down until his return to Russia in 1928. A work published in Berlin in 1922 [1] is remarkable for its frank utterances about the preceding years, and also because it has been omitted from the complete thirty-volume Soviet edition of Gorky's works. 'I have lived through and learned too much to have a right to be silent,' he wrote. He reconsidered in the light of his latest experience the character of the Russian peasant, superstitious, callous, cunning in methods of escape from administrative control, dreaming for centuries about a Government deprived of coercive power over its subjects. But the Civil War had focused his mind on a deep-rooted national characteristic, which oppressed him with foreboding.

'Long ago I read a book which bore the evil title, *Progress as the Evolution of Cruelty*. I read with anger, and did not then believe it, but now, after the terrifying madness of the European War and the bloody events of our own Revolution, these bitter paradoxes keep on returning to my memory. I must remark that in Russian cruelty there seems to have been no evolution whatsoever. Its forms, somehow, do not change. I think that the Russian people have an exclusive sense of cruelty (as exclusive as the Englishman's sense of humour), cold-blooded, as if testing by exact experiment how much pain human beings can endure. In Russian cruelty one feels a diabolical inventiveness, refined and *recherché*. Perhaps it was sharpened by traditional stories of Christian martyrs, perhaps by addiction to alcohol.' Nor is it confined to isolated pathological individuals, for it frequently shows collective enjoyment of torture. A seventeenth-century chronicler relates that in his time they sprinkled gunpowder in men's mouths or stuffed it in their buttocks and then blew them up. 'In 1918 and 1919 Russians did exactly the same in

[1] *O Russkom Krestyanstve*, Berlin, 1922

the Don and the Ukraine. They stuffed men with dynamite cartridges.'

In Siberia peasants would dig holes and bury Red Army prisoners, head downwards, leaving their legs sticking out up to the knees. They then gradually filled up the holes with earth, watching the convulsions of the victims, which of them took longest to die. They also skinned men alive, slowly. 'Which was crueller, the White or the Red? Probably both equally; in any case both were Russian. As to the question of degree, history will answer definitely, those were most cruel who were most active.'

Gorky also recorded illuminating conversations he had with men who took part in the Civil War. He asked some soldiers: 'Don't you feel upset, to go on killing one another?' 'No, not at all,' came the answer; 'he has a rifle, so have I. That means we are equal. Let us kill each other. Thus the earth will be disencumbered.' One Red Army soldier told him: 'Civil War hardly matters. But international war against foreigners weighs heavily on the soul. I tell you frankly, comrade, it comes easier to beat another Russian. We have so many people, such bad agriculture. Well, so we burn down a village. What does it matter? It would have burned down in any case some time. But when at the beginning of the war, I found myself in Prussia, my God, how sorry I felt for the people there! What a wonderful agriculture we ruined—for some unknown reason. When they wounded me, I was almost happy. . . .' I tried to tell this man something about Russia, her significance in the world. He listened to me thoughtfully, smoking a cigarette; then his eyes showed boredom. With a sigh he remarked: "Yes, of course, it used to be a special kind of power, quite unlike any others, but now to my mind it has fallen into the last stage of worthlessness." '

During the 1921 famine, calm and cynical peasants used to repeat the old proverb: 'One doesn't weep in Ryazan about the harvest failure in Pskov.' Many were glad that the weak and sick were dying off, leaving more food for the tougher survivors. They resented the townsman more than ever as a superfluous being, a parasite living on their blood and sweat. 'You made the revolution on your own account, and not for our benefit,' they said. 'If *we* had made the Revolution, it would long ago have been quiet on earth. We should have order. We ought to wipe out all the clever men, then we fools would find it easier to live.' A progressive peasant from Ryazan told him: 'We do not need any big factories, they produce nothing but quarrels and every kind of vice.' All the factories ought to be small, and situated at some distance from each other. Every province should be autonomous.

One bearded young man remarked to him: 'You have learned to fly in the air like crows, to swim under water like pike, but you don't know how to live like human beings on earth. We should first settle ourselves firmly on the ground, and only afterwards in the air. Why waste so much money on all those pastimes?' In the famine, a peasant killed a Bashkir who had slaughtered his cow, and then seized the Bashkir's cow. He expected to be punished for the theft, but felt no responsibility for the murder. An insignificant human life was cheaper than a valuable animal.

Pondering over these encounters, no wonder that Gorky felt grim forebodings about the next phase in the conflict, the protracted civil war between the Russian village and the town. He asked it to be set on record, for his endless foreign questioners, that he neither judged nor justified anybody. He explained the ugliness of the Revolution as a stubborn fact, an outcome of the exhausting European war, the breakdown of authority, and of the ingrained cruelty of the half-savage Russian people. He foretold that the next generation could hardly be expected to bring forth more sympathetic individuals, but rather harshly practical men of affairs, appreciating the value of electricity, tractors, and soil-science, but remaining equally suspicious of any townsman educated beyond the range of their immediate material needs.

Later he denounced the 'odious hypocrisy' of those self-righteous European moralists, who said they shuddered over the bloody ferocity of the Russian Revolution, yet during the four years of international European butchery allowed millions of their best young men to be maimed or killed for no convincing reason.

He chose to regard this conduct and its aftermath as a sign that the more civilized Western nations were also sinking back into a moral barbarism, of which Russia was not the sole example. Instead of purging and purifying the survivors, the malignant sufferings of the war seemed to have soured and shrivelled many people.

XII

SECOND EXILE

THOUGH Lenin had half implored, half ordered him to go abroad for medical treatment, Gorky's departure from Russia in 1921 was not entirely due to failing health. His independent stand had made for him some bitter enemies among the Soviet bureaucrats. He was on the worst possible terms with Zinoviev, the Party chief of Leningrad, who had gone so far as threatening to search Gorky's apartment and to arrest his associates. In 1922 he collaborated with the poet, Khodasevich, in founding a journal called *Besyeda* (published in Berlin), which optimistically attempted to blend contributions from Soviet Russian writers with articles from intelligent Russian *émigrés*. In this arduous undertaking the latter element inevitably predominated. But in the early nineteen-twenties some writers, who later returned to Russia, Alexei Tolstoy, Byely, Pilnyak, and Nikitin, were still living or travelling abroad.

Seven issues of this journal appeared under Gorky's editorship, but not a single one of them was allowed to be sold across the Soviet boundary, despite his struggles and impassioned protests. Gorky tried to force the issue by writing indignantly to Moscow that he would not contribute another line to any Soviet journal until *Besyeda* was admitted. Even that threat had no effect. He heard that the 'wise and mighty' men in Moscow had decided that he would more probably return to Russia if *Besyeda* was still banned there. 'But he won't go back,' Gorky wrote angrily. 'He is stubborn too.' He added his comment that already Soviet officialdom could allow no *a-political* expression on any subject whatsoever, 'for it no longer recognizes the existence of any people not infected with politics from their cradles'. [1]

[1] *Harvard Slavic Studies*, 1953, vol. 1, p. 291.

In Sorrento he often worked ten hours a day. His royalties, which still came from Russia, with smaller sums from the outside world, enabled him to live in modest comfort and to support his various dependants. News from Russia, though he could hardly live without it, rarely cheered him. In November 1923 he expressed incredulous horror at the latest Soviet *Guide on the removal of anti-artistic and counter-revolutionary literature from libraries serving the mass-reader*, which consigned to the index of forbidden books (to mention only the most important ones) the works of Plato, Kant, Schopenhauer, V. Solovyov, Taine, Ruskin, Nietzsche, and L. Tolstoy. He wrote that he seriously thought of renouncing his Soviet citizenship in protest against such 'intellectual vampirism'. But that impulse soon subsided. His national roots remained stronger than his anger against Bolshevik crimes. Moreover, a rupture with the Soviet Government would have deprived him of substantial royalties, which he received from the sale of his books in Russia.

He found the Southern Italian climate soothing, and the people friendly. 'You know, it is the holiday season here,' he wrote to Khodasevich in 1924. 'Almost every day there are fireworks, processions, music, and popular celebrations. And at home? I think. And—forgive me—I am overcome to the point of tears by envy, anguish, disgust, and everything else.' He said he felt so discouraged that, when he was alone at night, if it weren't so banal and ridiculous, he would have shot himself. Meanwhile he read a number of European novels, enough to revise momentarily his low opinion of contemporary Western writers. For in another letter to Khodasevich, he suddenly praised European literature 'as a remarkable and unique phenomenon. It sees everything, understands everything, and can talk about everything courageously and honestly. It is almost like an *all-seeing eye*.'[1]

In 1926, however, he pounced on his friend, the Russian writer, Vyacheslav Ivanov, for daring to call Soviet literature *provincial*. Was that any longer true, he asked, if one compared it, not with the past, but with the contemporary standard of

[1] Op. cit., p. 318.

European literature? 'I used to think for a long time, that in art we were inferior to Western Europeans, but today I begin to doubt it. The French have now reached the stage of Marcel Proust, who can write thirty lines, without a single punctuation mark, about utter trivialities. All their authors write alike, and they are all equally boring, colourless, and feeble.' [1] Clearly Gorky's contradictory judgements on the latest European literature should not be taken at their face value, or isolated from their context. While he came across a lot of printed rubbish, and promptly condemned it, we also hear that he admired Sinclair Lewis, Aldous Huxley, some of H. G. Wells and Hemingway. But, in one of the last letters he wrote, he said he felt gratified that the thousands of detective novels by Edgar Wallace and his breed, with their cheap blend of excitement and brutality, could hardly help to fortify the low morale of the European bourgeois, any more than sickly erotic ravings like D. H. Lawrence's *Lady Chatterley's Lover*. (Letter to V. Ivanov, 10 January 1936.)

The first major work of fiction produced by Gorky during his second European exile corresponded to his autobiographical series in taking a retrospective shape. *The Artamonov Business* (first published in 1925) returns to his documentary problem novels of the merchant class, but now more tersely designed to lead up to the October Revolution as a natural *dénouement*. As early as 1902 Gorky had spoken to Tolstoy about his desire to write an imaginative history covering three generations of a Russian merchant family, 'in which the law of degeneration operated mercilessly'. Tolstoy had keenly encouraged him, but, as often happens, the final execution of this project deviated substantially from the original intention.

Some Marxian critics were satisfied that the novel managed to demonstrate what they called the historical laws governing the growth of Russian capitalism, and the historical inevitability of its downfall. That judgement sounded satisfactory enough for people who never troubled to read or judge the novel for themselves. But, in fact, Gorky's elaborate human chronicle gave no

[1] Aleksinsky, op. cit., p. 211.

precise schematic explanation of recent Russian social history. It showed rather the fluidity of classes (the founder of the Artamonov family business was himself a liberated serf) and the many-sided unpredictable character of members of the Russian merchant class, which, even in its degenerate aspects, coloured the mentality of every other class, especially the factory artisans.

Moreover, Russian merchants were native products, *sui generis*, hardly comparable with the cold bourgeois blood-sucker of Marxian fame—largely drawn from the darkest side of Western Europe in the mid-nineteenth century. As Gorky himself remarked: 'The features distinguishing our big bourgeoisie from that of the West are clear and plentiful. Our historically younger bourgeois, springing as a rule from the peasantry, got rich quicker and more easily than the historically older bourgeois of the West. Our industrial magnate, untrained by the fierce competition prevailing in the West, preserved in himself, almost to the twentieth century, traits of the eccentric and the playboy.'

In some respects the subject-matter of *The Artamonov Business* lacks originality. Heavy merchants working like horses, then plunging into unrestrained debauch, naked prostitutes dancing on grand pianos, a hunchbacked brother retiring to the monastery in order to pray away the sins of his family—these were all sincerely poetic themes of the eighteen-seventies, but already exhaustively treated by Dostoyevsky, and worn thin by repeated handling. They provided excellent raw material for exciting literary art, but normal people were getting tired of them in actual life. Boborykin's sensitive psychological novels already showed merchant families in a more modern, sober, and sympathetic light.

Gorky's wide range spanning three generations in this family chronicle, enabled him to introduce a few twentieth-century types, but the bulk of the novel is devoted to the preceding generation. Though it is one of the liveliest novels he wrote, evidently the work palled on him, for he noted severely while he was writing it: 'If there is any place where they award prizes for dullness, I shall win first prize.'

The founder of the textile business, the ex-serf Ilya, a man of terrific physical energy, spared himself no effort, and tried to inspire his sons with his own passion for hard work. He was succeeded by his clumsy good-natured son, Peter, who worked from a sense of duty, but without enthusiasm, and by his nephew, Alexei (his sister-in-law's illegitimate son from a nobleman), skilful and self-confident, 'with the keen eyes of a hawk'. Since this second generation dominates the book, the reader has ample material to judge how far, and in what manner, it fell below its predecessor.

The figure of Peter emerges, on the whole, as a worried but conscientious slave of his own inherited factory. It is true that he committed a crime. He accidentally killed a repulsive and sickly boy, when he kicked him in a fit of temper, and he never admitted his responsibility. But in other ways he was more sinned against than sinning, and received scanty moral or material support from his own relatives. His hunchback brother had become a monk, but a sceptical one; his wife was hardly more than a good domestic animal; his cousin, Alexei, liked travelling to Moscow, and left the drudgery of routine management to Peter. Finally his son, Ilya, the apple of his eye, refused to take any part in the family business, departed to study history and to join, in some vague way, the 'revolutionary party'. That blow cut the last solid ground from under him and drove the old father (understandably enough) to forget his loneliness and disappointment in debauch.

Alexei represents the politically-minded business executive, now fully conscious that the middle class has replaced the aristocracy in power, and may soon be obliged to supplant the Tsar, if the Tsar cannot be turned into an alert and efficient business manager. He plans to be elected to the *Duma* because he is determined to convert his wealth into effective political power. His private life is happy, with a devoted and co-operative wife and a scientific son, Miron, in whom he sees a worthy successor. He collects beautiful old furniture and fine porcelain and tries to spend his money in a civilized way. Gorky, who also loved to

surround himself with works of art, rather gratuitously mocks
Alexei for indulging 'an absurd greed for unnecessary things'.
But, however hard he tried, his original intention to portray a
plainly degenerate type is even less convincingly fulfilled in the
keen energetic figure of Alexei than in the clumsy conscientious
Peter. Both are live and capable characters, victims of circumstances beyond their control.

The third generation is more cursorily characterized than the
two preceding ones, but it has taken a step forward in degeneration, though not to the extent of becoming incapable of managing
its business affairs. Yakov and Miron are simply paler con-
tinuations of their more robust fathers. The former is cynical and
sensual, much lazier than Peter, and without his sense of duty.
Miron has Alexei's alert intelligence but not a spark of his father's
passion; he abstains from all erotic adventures and marries for
money the doll-like daughter of a millionaire cotton-merchant.
But though he is a cold, self-centred prig, his education makes
him an efficient calculating machine and a cunning democrat. He
knows how to squeeze his old uncle out of effective management
of the business, and he jokes and curries favour with the factory
artisans in order to win their votes for his election to the *Duma*.

The average reader, not pre-conditioned by revolutionary zeal,
will hardly be convinced that the decline of this family of factory
managers adequately explains or justifies the October Revolution,
which, far from emerging as a natural *dénouement* of the preceding
action, suddenly bursts upon the story from outside, like a *deus
ex machinae*. The factory workmen (presumably the liberating
class, on which all future hope depends) are sketchily delineated,
without a single vivid personality among them, except the gay
old carpenter, Serafim, who drinks with Peter, and sings comic
songs. If Gorky wanted to show that the industrial middle class,
so promising and energetic in its hard-working infancy, became
boring, slack, and shallow, within two generations after its secure
establishment in power, then he partially succeeded, though even
the third generation produced Miron, the efficient engineer. On
the other hand, he failed to convey any compensating sense of

invigoration or renewal derived through the revolt of the artisan class, which he depicts as shifty and sordid, degenerating *pari passu* with their own masters, whose vices they have absorbed, without acquiring their sense of responsibility and order.

Peter's disturbing impression of his own factory workers can hardly be ascribed to class prejudice. It seemed to him that they were growing weaker, losing their robust peasant power of endurance, and, infected with chronic irritability, perpetually took offence without due cause and indulged in impudent threats against their employers. An undisciplined, unstable agitation spread among them. 'Formerly, in his father's day, they had lived more like a family, friendlier, drinking less, indulging less shamelessly in vice. But now their feelings had grown confused; they had become more aggressive and, it seemed, more intelligent, and yet they were increasingly careless in their work, more personally vindictive, and watched each other like calculating rogues.'

Gorky's picture of the workmen finally taking over the factory after the revolution is also hardly flattering to them. Their leader, Zakhar Morozov, made a new *proletarian order* in the nationalized workshop. He condemned three lads for stealing cloth, called them 'swine, stealing from themselves and from all of us', and ordered them to be beaten. Two other workmen joyfully lashed them with willow-canes. 'Like a big dog who has learned to walk on his hind legs', Zakhar then strutted about in imitation of the fat assistant district police-officer, and the workmen followed him like sheep.

The least blurred of these amorphous characters is the sinister gardener and porter, Tikhon. He has matured as a mental rebel against his lifelong employers, nursing all his grievances in silence, but waiting patiently for the appointed day of his revenge. When the Revolution finally overthrew the Artamonovs, Tikhon could at last speak out to the sick and pathetic old Peter. 'The war is against *you*,' he proclaimed; 'the last war. . . . I understood it before anybody else. I said, there will be penal servitude for everybody, and so it has turned out. . . . Countless crimes I watched, and used to wonder: When will the end come? Now *your* end has come. ... You Artamonovs killed my faith. For you have neither God nor Devil. ... You lived by fraud.' Throughout the sequence of the novel, mystery and suspense have accumulated round the figure of the silent Tikhon. Yet when at last he starts to speak, it is solely to release his pent-up hatred of the Artamonov family (who have always treated him quite kindly), and the mystery of his singular personality remains unsolved. Since this *grand finale* turns into a blatant anti-climax, the nemesis which overtakes the Artamonovs is strangely devoid of any tragic grandeur or sense of the inevitable. Perhaps Tikhon was merely a sullen blockhead, or a sphinx without a secret, but, if so, why did Gorky force on him a role beyond his powers? He never intended Tikhon to be a mere vehicle of accumulated petty grievances and impotent personal spite, yet he failed to bring his character to life by incarnating some constructive strivings.

Notes from a Diary (published 1924) holds a most important place in Gorky's unique autobiographical series. It excelled in brilliant character sketches of many strange and striking people whom he had met in Russia, and it vindicated his claim that he was fully equipped to write the plain unvarnished truth, when he set out to do so. For it combined a terse journalistic *reportage* with subtle mastery of atmosphere and uncanny pathos. He intended to call it, *A Book About Russian People as they used to be*, but later rejected that title as too pretentious. He summed up his attitude to them on a nostalgic note: 'I cannot feel definitely whether I want these people to be different. Wholly alien to nationalism, patriotism, and similar sicknesses of spiritual vision, at the same time I see them as exceptionally, fantastically, talented and original. ... Even fools in Russia are original ... in the intricacy and unexpectedness of their convolutions, Russians provide the most grateful material for an artist.'

Here are pre-eminently 'people for anecdotes'; the penniless but superstitious student, who inherited houses in Nijni Novgorod, and worried himself to death, because he had done nothing to deserve such an abundance of good luck; the old antique dealer, who believed that a giant spider had been sent by God to watch over his borrowed soul; the misanthropic ship's surgeon, who learned from his travels that man seems even more of a nonentity at sea than he is on land, and admired the Chinese custom of drowning superfluous children, like kittens, at birth; the established doctor, who quarrelled with his wife because she insisted that he should wear braces, then broke away from settled society because he craved for the unexpected, lashed out against modern culture as a morass of sentimental humbug, and behaved himself with the gay fury of a schoolboy, who, after finishing his course, tears up the textbooks; the strangely characteristic things people do when they are 'alone with themselves'; the top-hatted English clown bowing respectfully to his own image in a mirror; Tolstoy asking a lizard, basking on a warm stone, whether he is happy; Chekhov, sitting in his Yalta garden, trying to catch a sunbeam with his hat, then telling him that Balmont wrote, 'The sun smells of aromatic herbs', but here it only smells of Tartar sweat.

Gorky had written previously about the vast views, and wide majestic rivers, which gave solemnity and melancholy charm to the otherwise monotonous Russian landscape. But here, in *The Little Town*, he managed to laugh at the provincial Russian patriot, who went into raptures about the glorious expanse of the dreary and depressing Russian countryside, and exclaimed, gazing at the sky, that there are no stars anywhere like Russian stars, and that the Russian potato, too, is the finest in the world, where taste is concerned.

The more substantial sketches are of real historic characters. The Old Believer millionaire, Bugrov, owner of forests, flour-mills, and fleets, the merchant prince of Nijni Novgorod, impressed Gorky by his primitive energy and free creative mind. He described him with a sympathy far removed from that standard denigration of the *bourgeois*, which he glibly repeated in his later propagandist articles. A lavish philanthropist, Bugrov showered gifts on his native town. He gave it schools, fine new administrative buildings, and paid for its whole piped water supply. After having met Nicolas II a few times, and observed his feeble amiability, he came to the shrewd conclusion that Tsars were due to vanish from the contemporary scene, since they were no longer stern or fierce enough to hold their own. 'A Tsar,' said Bugrov, 'can only remain a ruler so long as he is terrifying.' Sovereigns, who inspire no awe, fail to fulfil their function. Gorky's barber in Arzamas had expressed a kindred view when he remarked: 'Terror for the soul is like a Turkish bath for the body—most invigorating.'

While Bugrov welcomed the limited usefulness to industry of recent scientific inventions, he saw with alarm how the innately superstitious peasants were disintegrating morally from the abrupt impact on their minds of telephones, gramophones, and mechanically propelled vehicles. He remembered one peasant who starved himself to death because of bewilderment after he had heard a well-known sacred song played on a gramophone. And he described how soon afterwards the people in this man's village began to spread wild rumours about *the devil in a box*, the arrival of Anti-Christ, and the approaching end of the world; many became incurable drunkards.

Bugrov expressed keen admiration for the character of Mayakin in Gorky's novel, *Foma Gordeyev*. In some ways he resembled Mayakin. He explained that he could see no sense in the current agitation to secure for Russia a parliamentary constitution, which, by mixing the common people too closely in the complicated mess of political manoeuvre and intrigue, would only confuse and soil their minds, while distracting their energy from their daily work. But he urged that far more honorific encouragement ought to be given to outstanding feats of labour, in order to distinguish efficient workers from inferior or lazy ones. 'I would like to award crosses and decorations for manual work,' he said, 'to carpenters, mechanics and artisans.'

In his almost religious reverence for exceptional achievements by skilled labourers, in his desire to give the slovenly or ignorant a shining example to emulate, the bourgeois millionaire, Bugrov, might be termed an ideal Bolshevik, and he proved how some sensible Bolshevik ideas were in fact derived from enterprising and far-sighted members of the Russian middle class. The other big industrial magnate described by Gorky, Savva Morozov, came much closer to the Social Democrats than Bugrov. He is introduced in the same sketch, complaining bitterly about the disastrous technical conservatism of the peasantry, the gross self-indulgence and lack of foresight shown by the merchant class. He gave Gorky money for promoting Social Democratic propaganda, and talked about the inevitability of Revolution.

The monarchist, V. Breyev, told Gorky about his mounting anger against the pedantic rationalism which blinded the educated rebels. The people needed a permanent mystery, not a new formula, he contended, for no state could ever be securely founded on a set of naked propositions. The only freedom which the people could enjoy with impunity would remain freedom of imagination. Apart from bread and circuses, they needed heroes and efficient leaders, whom they could admire and love without reserve. Therefore, the more inscrutable, remote, and inaccessible these heroes were, the less they were known or gossiped about as ordinary mortals, the greater the peoples' imaginative freedom, and the more spiritual comfort they would derive from it. That was a law of the human psyche which ought to be respected.

Gorky saw in Breyev a feverish manifestation of that same national *mystique*, which the Bolsheviks would know how to capture and employ for their own advantage. On the other hand, the disappointed revolutionary, Borisov, watched the triumphant common people after 1917, still seething with anger and revenge, but spiritually empty and exhausted, left without faith in their own further transformation. After a lifetime of fighting for their cause, he now found himself a complete stranger to them, as if, he said, Columbus, after all his hardships, 'had discovered America, only to find that America disgusted him'. He saw that everybody was busily absorbed in making a revolution, 'even people who do not know how to sew a button on their trousers'.

Another essay, *The Murderers* (published 1926), provides a truthful commentary on an ugly by-product of modern social change—the spread of violent or abnormal crime, plus the un-healthy public interest aroused by it. Gorky, prior to 1917, investigated the crime statistics of the population covered by the circuit of the Moscow law courts. He was appalled by the number of murders and sexual attacks, such as violation of women and rape of minors.

Apart from the mounting quantity and squalor of modern crimes, he remarked that many contemporary murderers had come to esteem themselves, like sportsmen trying to break established records; if one murderer cut his corpse into six pieces, the next would cut his into twenty. He did not doubt that popular newspapers promoted violent crime by revelling in succulent descriptions of it, by making the murderer a hero and his crime a feat of courage, showing a morbid thrill about the criminal's dexterity or brutal daring, together with a blank cynical in-difference to his unlucky victim. It would be healthier and wiser, Gorky urged, to create round murderers an atmosphere of silent oblivion, checking any sharp curiosity about their personalities and actions. In describing the murderers he had met and spoken to, Gorky said he was painfully struck by their blunt stupidity, conceit, and self-importance. Only one of them, a handsome pack-horse driver, with an uncanny smile, who murdered from uncontrollable impulse and curiosity, was intelligently aware of his predicament. 'You fools,' he cried, when he was captured, 'you ought to bind my soul, and not my hands.' And he told the judge: 'You must punish me severely, your Honour, punish me with death—or else . . . I can't live with people, even in jail. I've got a crime against my soul . . . and then more people will have to suffer for it. You must exterminate me, sir.'

Then the unchecked spread of detective stories and gangster films promoted a state of moral stupor. 'If an idiot cuts his neigh-bour to pieces and eats him, all the newspapers will write about this remarkable idiot for a whole month. He finds himself the centre of public attention. But when the great surgeon, Appel, three times brings back to life, by massage of the heart, people who had died on the operating table, nobody either knows or writes about it.' Thus people's minds were doped by nerve-racking and destructive stimulants, while their deeper constructive emotions and desires grew blunt or atrophied.

Gorky's own mind was moving in protest towards the opposite extreme. He grasped at salvation in the rarefied and incredible *purity* of the pre-censored Soviet Press, which bans any reference to private theft, murder, or sexual offences. It did not worry him that such a policy might produce an elevated official dullness, a stilted hypocrisy, which would make the public less keen on reading or believing newspapers at all. He trusted that a respectably dull, informative Press would, at any rate, diminish the morbid excitement aroused by crime, and even help to foster the edifying illusion that such crimes were vanishing from the Soviet sector of the earth.

While Gorky continued to show high creative powers during this period of voluntary exile, his best writings became more and more retrospective chronicles of a vanished age, and he dealt with the disagreeable present only in analytical or stridently denunciatory articles. But, as the years passed by in exile, he began to feel a growing nostalgia for his native land—reinforced by diminishing doubts about the staying-power of its Bolshevik rulers. Sorrento, with all its natural charms and gentle climate, was far from the centre of world affairs. He felt cut off and useless there, and he dreaded a lonely and futile old age. Exile, however peaceful and comfortable, stimulated Gorky's incurable restlessness. And seen from afar, through the softening mists of memory, Russia began to appear to him brighter and more alluring. The base intrigue and petty personal spite, indulged in by so many Russian *émigrés*, depressed him, and modern Europe bored him. 'If you only knew how naked Europe has become, and what a cold shamelessness has taken possession of people,' he wrote to his friend, the author, Sergeyev-Tsensky. 'It is remarkable that now suicides take place for more and more trivial reasons. A few days ago in Paris, a man put a bullet through his head merely because he had forgotten how to knot his tie.' [1]

---

[1] *Sobraniye Sochineniy*, vol. 30, p. 41.

Then his active ex-wife, who lived in Moscow, started to urge Gorky to return to Russia. She wrote to her son, Max, who lived somewhat idly with his father, that he could also find a useful job if he returned. Gorky remarked of her that a politically obsessed woman can behave like an enraged canary. But one of his last letters to his colleague, Khodasevich, showed the direction in which his mind was moving. 'Of course I can't agree with you,' he argued, 'that there is no will to work in Russia today. We have more will to work than there is anywhere in modern Europe.'[1] He persuaded himself that, whatever their initial crimes and blunders, the Bolsheviks were vigorous educable people, who had not yet succumbed to 'that boundless cynicism' which made life in the West so horrible and stifling to him. He flattered himself that the masters of the new Russia would be glad to learn from him, might benefit from his guidance. He renounced the aphorism which he had formerly proclaimed, 'Those born to crawl can never learn to fly'.

He measured the decline of the West by the apparent taste of its majority in music; 'that modern Western "evolution" from the beauty of the minuet, the lively grace of the waltz, to the coarse fox-trot and jerky spasms of the charleston, from Mozart and Beethoven, to the negro jazz-band, whose black performers must laugh inwardly, watching how their white masters evolve into savages.' ('About the Music of the Fat', *Pravda*, 1928).

---

[1] *Harvard Slavic Studies*, p. 332, Harvard, 1954.

XIII

THE SOVIET LAUREATE

WHEN Gorky decided to make his compact with the Soviet regime, he knew that he would have to take final and irrevocable monastic vows. He had seen too much of the Revolution at close quarters to be deluded by any other people's fairy-tales about it. He preferred his own version, bad as it was, and piously hoped that Russian officialdom had grown less mentally static. Apart from that, only in Russia did his reputation as a writer stand established on a firm foundation. The Government courted his favour and the public bought his books. He was in growing demand and might still play a major constructive part there, while in the West he remained a solitary, ambiguous figure, with a precarious fame.

In 1928 he took the plunge, and returned to Moscow for the festive celebration of his sixtieth birthday. Filled with mixed emotions, his speech to the welcoming crowds was punctuated with sobs and tears. Special reception committees met him formally at every place he visited, as if he were an influential foreign potentate. He was also greeted as a saviour, bringing fresh hope, and besieged by pathetic petitioners, who expected him to work miracles at once. His home town, Nijni Novgorod, was shorn of its historic name and re-named Gorky in his honour. He was re-elected to the Academy of Sciences (from which he had been expelled in 1902) and the highest civilian decoration, the Order of Lenin, was conferred on him.

His material comfort was no less well provided for. In Moscow he received the luxurious, florid mansion of a former industrial magnate, together with a fine villa on the outskirts—and an ample supply of motor-cars, domestic staff, and private secretaries, all inevitably under the control of the Secret Police, who, though they coaxed and flattered him, remained responsible for guarding every step and watching every personal contact in the precious life of the *great proletarian writer.* Stalin believed that Gorky, like most men, had his price, and he therefore showered honours on him, but he underrated Gorky's perspicacity. To start with, he felt stimulated. 'Here everything burns and boils,' he wrote. 'It is a new people with a new psychology.' (*Pravda*, May 1928.) In 1929 he was taken on a grand conducted tour of Russia, and re-visited Astrakhan and Tiflis which he had known as a penniless young tramp.

Perhaps he felt a strained excess of uniformity in the stormy and unanimous applause with which selected deputations greeted him at every stopping-place; perhaps he resented the official veneration which shielded him so carefully from chance personal meetings with members of the public. For, after his return to Moscow, he started to walk the streets disguised as a coachman, wearing a false beard and with a hat pushed over his eyes. Like a Soviet Haroun Al Raschid, he tried to find out what ordinary people were saying among themselves about the burning topics of the day, entered clubs and restaurants *incognito*, and mixed with crowds in the market-place. He informed the State Publishing House that he was longing to write a substantial imaginative book about the new Russia, using material from his 1929 travel sketches, but it is significant that no such book ever materialized.

On the contrary, his literary work between 1928 and 1936 (the year of his death), although it was voluminous, added little that was either outstanding in quality or new in kind. Much of his activity took a monotonously critical or administrative shape. Like a superior schoolmaster defending a tradition, he continued to exhort young Soviet writers to learn from the classics of the previous century, and to reproach them for their clumsy, careless, or unconscientious work. He was persuaded by Stalin to organize the first Union of Soviet Writers. He wrote an unfinished and rambling novel, *Klim Samgin* (1927–36), about the Kazan intelligentsia before the Revolution, a number of short stories, and

I

some more plays about the old Russian middle class. One topical play, *Somov and Others*, was praised by Soviet critics for unmasking 'enemies of the people', but it was only published five years after Gorky's death.[1] The most original new work, directly related to the Soviet scene, was that strange product of collective authorship, which he edited, describing the construction of the Baltic–White Sea Canal by thousands of regenerated convicts.

It was not only the 'White Guard' *émigrés* who reproached him for becoming the dupe and sycophant of a government which needed his co-operation. A former socialist friend of his from Nijni Novgorod, Madame E. Kuskova, who had been expelled from Russia after serving on the Committee to help starving peasants during the 1921 famine, wrote from abroad to question him in some bewilderment. In 1929 he answered her in a detailed letter of self-justification which (whether one approves of it or not) had the merit of removing Gorky's motives from any further shadow of doubt.

He told his old friend with brutal frankness: 'You are accustomed to speak about facts which disgust you. For my part I not only count it my right to keep silent about them, but I consider the faculty to do so as one of my chief virtues. . . . Immoral, you will say. So be it. The fact is that I hate sincerely and inexorably the truth, which for ninety-nine per cent of people is an abomination and a lie. You probably know that during my stay in Russia I have raised my voice in public both in the Press and at meetings of comrades, against *self-criticism*, against that habit of upsetting and blinding men by the poisonous and fatal dust of everyday truth. Without success, of course, but that does not damp my ardour.

'That other truth, which excites in men confidence in their will and reason, is already sown in the minds of the masses, and its results are excellent. What is important for me is the rapid all-round development of human personality, the birth of a new man of culture, the workman in a sugar-refining factory reading Shelley in the original. . . . Such men do not need the petty

[1] Arkhiv M. Gor'khovo, vol. 2, *Piesy i Stsenariy*, Moscow–Leningrad, 1941.

accursed truth in the midst of which they are struggling. They need the truth they create for themselves. You may call me optimist, idealist, romantic, etc. That is your affair. Mine is to explain as well as I can, why I am now *unilateral*.' [1]

Gorky had travelled far from his chivalrous intervention to save exceptionally deserving and gifted men and women from sinking in the chaos of the Revolution. He had abandoned, as beyond his powers, that prolonged attempt to find some common ground, in sympathy or reason, to fill the widening gulf which divided the new Soviet intelligentsia from the non-communist *émigrés* and the more balanced section of the Western educated class. Having deliberately burned his boats in Europe, he now simplified the issue by reducing it to one abrupt alternative: 'If the enemy does not surrender, he will be exterminated.' With a new and arrogant national pride, he applied himself to advertising the brightly coloured official picture of the Soviet state, without worrying how far that picture came nearer to reality than a bare, abstract statement of unfulfilled *desiderata*.

Nevertheless Gorky, as a guide, philosopher, and loyal friend, still aiming instinctively at high artistic and educational standards, rather than at the promotion of compulsory political legends, continued to render valuable services to Russian culture. He helped to save the few remaining writers of intrinsic merit from being strangled by proletarian cliques, whose organized vulgarity, conceit, and collective petty tyranny, threatened to crush or silence all serious authors, who in self-defence remained aloof from them. He openly denounced cunning parasites, who had mastered little more than a smattering of Bolshevik jargon and intrigue, the idle hangers-on of Soviet publishing houses, who sought literary jobs, not because they had either talent or strong inclination, but because they wanted easy remunerative work, and found it glamorous to be considered *men of letters*. He warned over-sanguine or boastful literary *parvenus* that it was absurdly premature to expect the birth of any new literary masterpiece in the still crudely primitive Soviet Union.

---

[1] Quoted by G. Aleksinsky, op. cit., pp. 229–30.

He voiced disappointment and dismay at the needless increase in the number of literary critics who merely indulged in venomous disputes with each other, injecting a flavour of personal vanity and spite into almost everything they wrote. He felt repelled by so many dry official faces, or arrogant political masks, hiding hearts of stone. 'It is extremely sad and strange to see that the disputes of people, who agree on essentials, are carried on in such an embittered tone, filled with the coarsest personal abuse and without any trace of comradely feeling.' (*About Literature*, 1931.) Moreover, critics were so bleakly preoccupied with revolutionary pedagogics that they taught nothing about mastering the art of language. 'The articles of our young critics are outstanding for the abstract, anaemic, and deadly dryness of their language, for their addiction to empty names and scholastic verbiage.' (*Literary Pastimes*, 1935.)

He also warned the artisan class against being infected by the ordinary material cravings and habits of the bourgeoisie, although he saw that they were already carried away by them. The new *bourgeois communist* shocked the revolutionary idealist. 'Lenin, in talking about the right of the workman to inherit the achievements of culture, had in mind not only comfortable water-closets, but principally all science and technique which could preserve both the physical and moral health of people.'(*About Irresponsible People*, 1930.) But gangs of petty careerists sought only a physically comfortable place in the new regime, and found it by no worthier means than the adroit use of revolutionary phraseology and personal wire-pulling.

They used that sinister phrase, *Self-criticism*, and denunciation of other people, as weapons to promote their own advancement. 'The Soviet apparatus is badly burdened by wreckers of this kind, and equally by superfluous though resonant phrases about *cultural work*. . . . People keep on jumping up from below, concerned with one thing only, that others should see and hear them; they jump up, and soil, by their allegedly new but stale words, matters which should be simple and clear. . . . *This dust of words darkens our life.*' (*About Irresponsible People*, 1930.)

The working class was forced to spend so much energy in building up its ruined industry and trade, Gorky concluded, that only a few scraps of energy remained to undertake responsible work 'on the cultural front'. And yet without a lively interest in the past history of human art and thought nobody could become a cultured man today, and, without seriously studying the past, it was impossible either to grasp the sense of the present or feel the goals of the future.

Though Gorky dimly recognized that independent literature as a fine art was dead or dying, he preferred to regard that death as a temporary eclipse. And he quite inconsistently complained that the stirring events of the day evoked a disappointingly feeble echo from Soviet imaginative writers—a complaint which crowds of later Soviet critics repeated and elaborated *ad nauseam*. It was sad that the same giant industrial plans and social upheavals which excited politicians, failed to stir the hearts of imaginative writers, and that the new standard themes and up-to-date heroic types, for which the Party wanted high-pressure advertisement in literature, left many authors, and therefore readers, strangely cold, bored, and unresponsive. 'The hero of our day is the scientist, the inventor, the member of the Young Communist League, the Pioneer,' Gorky kept on urging. 'But our imaginative writers fail to notice them, or if they do, they merely envelop them in a cloud of soulless words.' (*About the Poet's Library*, 1931.)

The note of puritanical self-denial running through Gorky's appeals was pitched too high, for the aspiring Soviet bourgeoisie hardly appears to have been radically affected by it—not enough to save them, any more than their Western counterparts, from continuing to hanker after a cosy suburban nest, where tea could be served in red polka-dotted cups under the gentle glow of an orange lampshade. Despite the official Gorky cult, the persistent idealization of such eminently bourgeois scenes and settings is by no means banished from the modern Soviet novel.

But Gorky blamed the literary critic, as much as the new Soviet writers, for the prevailing poverty and weakness of Soviet literature. He accused Soviet critics of being 'inexcusably one-sided', of patronizing hurried slovenly work and encouraging young writers, without experience or discipline, to rush into print. Some of these, by cultivating a show of proletarian rough- ness and clumsy bombastic language, had won reputations which were ludicrously undeserved. The real life of a Soviet author, Gorky argued, should be so impregnated with epic severity that correspondingly robust qualities would find reflection in his work. If deeds were really so glorious (as they were said to be) they should inspire enough impressive words. In vain did the author cultivate long-winded abstruse verbal patterns or patriotic rhetoric, for his language should naturally emerge as simple, accurate, and strong as it had been among the nineteenth-century masters.

Sometimes, in the midst of his schoolmasterly or flamboyant exhortations, Gorky dropped a hint that he understood why Soviet spiritual life had sunk so low—through prolonged physical and mental overstrain, undernourishment, haunting fear, anxiety, and numbed absorption in the bare routine of industrial labour. 'A human being for the sake of mankind will be possible only in the future, when the distorting burden of all national, class, and religious obsessions no longer hampers the free growth of his strength and capacities. But until that time, so long as any class government exists, a man of letters, whether he wants to or not, is forced to serve the temporary interests of his epoch.' (*About Reality*, 1929.)

Gorky also tried hard to instil into new Soviet literature a per- manent sense of waging ideological warfare against its implacable enemy, the Western bourgeois world. 'Even the bourgeois world,' he complained, 'fails to arouse in our writers an appro- priately clear and satirical attitude to its astounding cynicism and manifold filth.' To lash up hatred and suspicion against virtually unknown foreigners is always an easier objective than to evoke a glow of admiration for home affairs, dimmed by intimate and daily familiarity. Yet evidently Soviet writers showed a culpable indifference to both these themes, or else a temperamental inability to do justice to them.

In fact only a few of the older authors, like Ilya Ehrenburg and

Alexei Tolstoy, had lived long enough abroad to write convincingly about any foreign countries, and they were the very ones who, after their return to Russia, found more security in writing about approved Russian themes. Neither did Gorky himself provide much factual information about the course of European affairs, though he at times described with relish the universal agitation and depression of the bourgeois, the feverish hunt for pleasure with which wealthy people tried to drown their fear of tomorrow, the abnormal craze for cheap excitement, the spread of sexual perversion, crime, and suicide.

He urged Russians, in no diplomatic language, to shake the dust of the old world from their feet, 'in order to escape from being infected by its poisonous decay'. (*How I Learned to Write*, 1928.) 'Have we not the right to hate these incurable degenerates and human deformities, this irresponsible international horde of criminals, who will certainly try to inflame their *nations* against that Government which is creating Socialism?' (*Proletarian Hatred*, 1935.) Gorky, like many propagandists, accused the foreign enemy of vices which he had amply observed in his native land. He tossed out choice terms of abuse, like 'biped scum', 'vermin in human shape', 'predatory greed of bloated spiders dressed in tattered rags of religion and philosophy'. And these became classic Soviet epithets. He enjoyed a gift for virulent invective. And he used it to adorn a *motif* which, with minor variations, still dominates the Soviet attitude towards obstinate foreigners who prefer to remain outside the Communist fold. But it seems that Gorky also signed many articles, drafted or rewritten for him by the Party editors. Finding himself ruthlessly exploited as a useful figure-head, he began to realize the quixotic folly of his old desire to 'educate' or convert his Bolshevik masters.[1] The tables had been turned.

While Gorky tirelessly poured out a stream of advisory articles to fortify young aspirants, he never achieved any synthesis of the Soviet period in his own imaginative work. His most constructive single contribution was a remarkable journalistic

---

[1] See *Mosty*, No. 1, Article by T. Shub, *M. Gorky*, New York, 1959.

experiment. It emerged in the bulky but now almost forgotten volume about the building of the Baltic–White Sea Canal, which he inspired and edited.[1] This book served an important dual purpose: to vindicate the new theory of *collective authorship*, and to prove that feats of Soviet labour and enthusiasm for hard manual work were not figments of propagandist brains, but genuine phenomena, which could be revealed through documentary literature. Gorky persuaded thirty-four professional authors to contribute to this composition, which gave the inside story of a vast Soviet corrective labour camp. The names of every individual author were appended to the chapters which they wrote.

It is stated that in the construction of this Canal a mere thirty-seven police officials organized the work of thousands of criminals and political prisoners, belonging to a multitude of races and speaking many different tongues—'a fine outfit to *overtake America*,' as one of the prisoners remarked. Comrade Yagoda aimed at transforming the camp into a construction *collective*. All these *enemies of society*, whether consciously anti-Soviet or merely anti-social, were forcibly drawn together in a huge enterprise, visibly and incontestably *useful* to everybody. Here they were taught to direct their old accumulated anger against other human beings into a more exhilarating fight against stubborn stones and marshes. The bold and difficult undertaking, and the literary account of it, were planned to demonstrate, both a dazzling victory of organized human energy over harsh intractable obstacles, and a return to *civic health* on the part of socially 'sick' and dangerous people, testified to by their own admissions. It appears that thousands of former thieves, crooks, wreckers, and *saboteurs* were rapidly transformed into co-operative, keen, and efficient colleagues. Though we are given brilliant psychological detail about the process of their individual conversion, we are not told for how long afterwards this state of grace endured. But hard labour is presented as the sole reliable psychiatrist.

---

[1] *Byelomorsko-Baltiysky Kanal imeni Stalina*, Moscow, 1934.

Since most of the workmen are not yet articulate enough to speak for themselves, professional writers must interview and interpret them, so that the world may know their hidden feelings. Gorky had always excelled in this technique. 'Frankly, my life would make a dozen novels,' says the ex-thief, Kvasnitsky. 'I've avoided work as a duke, a travelling salesman, as a surgeon, a violinist, and a Roman Catholic monk. For thirty years I was a thief, though my real profession is tanning. . . . Thieves are usually capable. A fool gets caught on the first job. Now I'm watching a Leningrad bandit here. The boy is twenty-one years old. He's been working in camp a week, and every day he works worse. . . . I showed him newspaper cuttings with pictures of Kovalev and other *shock-workers*. I asked him what he could do. It turned out that the boy can draw. That night we put a *wall-newspaper* together. He drew caricatures of the shirkers and laughed with pleasure.'

One former *kulak*, who has seen the light, is reported to have said about his stern but benevolent G.P.U. organizers: 'It used to be a lot of fine talk, and in fact thieving and drunkenness. But now the new bosses follow a different line; though they are dressed like officers, they live like monks.' The popular humorist, Zoschenko, who also collaborated, shaped the manuscript of a former notorious international crook, called Abraham Rotten-berg, who was serving a long-term penal sentence. This man's exemplary industry in the camp earned his release and the title, *honoured worker*; he went on to take part in the building of the Moscow–Volga Canal. Zoschenko disarmingly began his account of moral rehabilitation thus (chapter 12): 'To tell the truth, I approached this affair myself with some scepticism, but I turned out to be extraordinarily mistaken.'

The first-class engineer, Maslov, was ready to suffer stoically for his anti-Soviet political ideals, in the wilderness to which he had been condemned, surrounded by riff-raff. But he was instructed to design lock-gates in wood, without a scrap of metal, and he had to solve this novel problem. The stimulus of invention, the furious tempo of the whole enterprise, we are told, spurred him on to design fifteen variants, and finally to find a correct solution. After the Canal was completed, Maslov was rewarded by receiving the Order of the Red Banner, and then he soon shed his air of martyrdom and his former laconic, grudging manner.

The story of the formerly wealthy bourgeois engineer, Alexander Ananyev, whose zealous work on the Canal later qualified him as a *shock-worker* at Byelomorstroy, contains a fascinating retrospective picture of feverish expanding big business in the years before the Revolution, and illustrates the almost unbroken continuity of Russian economic penetration into Central Asia, before and after 1917. Military defeat by Japan in the Far East greatly accelerated Russian economic activity in quarters where it met with less resistance.

Ananyev had promoted a company for the irrigation of the Shirabad valley, and travelled to that vassal Khanate of the Russian Empire, where Russian citizens enjoyed extra-territorial rights. He described the characteristic group of passengers bound for Turkestan, gathered together on the saloon-deck of the paddle-steamer—naval officers banished for Homeric debauchery to serve in the Amu-Daria fleet, diplomatic officials accredited to the courts of the 'independent' Emir of Bokhara and Khan of Khiva, priests serving garrison churches, young Bokhara merchants who had travelled to learn the current forms of social polish in the *cafés chantants* of St. Petersburg and Moscow, middle-aged lionesses, hostesses of the *demi-monde*, seeking adventure, easy money, and valuable gifts from dissipated Emirs.

This book undoubtedly achieved its purpose by presenting at least one real forced labour camp in strangely glowing colours. It even struck an authentic Dostoyevskyan note, in the mood which it conveyed of personal willingness to accept and enjoy the hardest labour as a merited form of penance for a wicked or stupidly wasted life. It emphasized the hopeful *possibilities* of labour camps, compared with the worse alternatives of deliberate or enforced idleness, chronic crime, or passive destitution. As a lively and clear chronicle of a peculiar social experiment, coloured by the temporary enthusiasm of gifted writers, the stories are unique, and can still be read with profit. But they were not destined to open up a new source of collective literary creation, as Gorky hoped; and it would be absurd to judge them as factual descriptions, applicable to any average labour camp.

Although the enterprising Ministry of the Interior embarked on a growing number of gigantic forced-labour projects in the following years, no similar books appeared to edify the public. Makarenko's *The Road to Life* (1934) might be claimed as an exception, for it also described the poignant revivalist emotions said to have been generated in a penal settlement. But this book is mainly valuable as the record of an enthusiastic pedagogue. It concentrated on the drastic methods which Makarenko devised in Soviet penal training centres, which shepherded together the millions of homeless and often criminal waifs and strays (created by the civil war), and re-shaped them by severe training into tolerable citizens.

Gorky pressed for documentary moral tales because he saw no alternative for Soviet authors. But he remained aware that this kind of writing might be read today and used tomorrow for wrapping soap. Hence his loyalty to the monumental literature of the nineteenth century, which brought him closer to the sceptical E. Zamyatin, who frankly wrote: 'I fear that we shall get no genuine literature until we have cured ourselves of a new Catholic Orthodoxy, which no less than the old fears every heretical word. If that sickness is incurable—I fear that Russian literature will have only one future—its past.'[1]

---

[1] E. Zamyatin, *Litsa*, p. 189, New York, 1955.

XIV

THE TEACHER OF SOVIET
NATIONAL ADVERTISING METHODS

DESPITE his devastating criticism of many Soviet failings, Gorky is responsible for launching the most impressive sequence of ideas, elaborated later to advertise the Soviet state, both for its historical inevitability, its noble aspirations, and its achievements in the realm of fact. He provided a convenient summary of these ideas (although he hardly broke fresh ground) in his famous speeches to the first Congress of Soviet Writers (1934). His main speech, though lucid and vigorous in its attempt to re-establish standards and aims for bewildered Soviet writers, is strangely distorted and meagre in its handling of the past, despite the fact that it emphatically returns to the past for present guidance.

In his strained effort to link rustic legend with modern industrial labour, he started by pointing out that historians of ancient culture had paid inadequate attention to folk-lore, to the unwritten imaginary compositions of illiterate people. He went on to assert that the chief hidden motive underlying all these fairy-tales is the perpetual striving of men to lighten their labour and simultaneously to make it more productive. He illustrated this sweeping generalization by a few superficially plausible instances. People dreamed of speedier movement, therefore they created legends in which they flew through the air on magic carpets, or walked in seven-league boots. They longed to grasp and enjoy the fruits of arduous labour by quick and easy methods, if not by miracles. Thus in their tales they built magnificent palaces in a single night, and brought back the dead to life by sprinkling them with enchanted water.

Gorky argued that beneath all these fancies, lay genuine

technical thoughts, which could only have arisen in the minds of men who performed manual work. For their minds were inextricably linked with the manual processes which they performed in life. So, he said, would those of the philosopher, Immanuel Kant, have been if, barefoot, and clothed in an animal's skin, he had been denied the fatal opportunity of severing his thought from his hands, and cogitating at his writing-desk about the *thing in itself*!

Of course this arbitrary interpretation, valid within limits, falls short of justifying Gorky's foregone conclusion. It entirely omits love and adventure stories, and many charming fables, which in no way depend for their effect on the lure of magic labour-saving devices. And Gorky never considered that even the tale of the flying carpet might have originated from a non-technical but natural motive, the desire to fly away from a painful and arduous routine and seek refuge in a refreshing world of unimpeded fantasy.

There is more ground for Gorky's other main contention, that pre-Christian folk-lore never suffered from superfluous reflection on metaphysical fundamentals or first causes. This sickly and fruitless deviation, he claimed, started with speculative thinkers, like Plato, a forerunner of some Christian philosophers, who all tried to explain the world and the growth of human ideas in abstract terms, divorced from deeper desires and physical work. Gorky again contemptuously swept his favourite victim, Kant, into this camp of futile philosophers.

Perhaps he had never dipped into that formidable volume, *The Critique of Pure Reason*, for he failed to observe that Kant, with all his cloudy Teutonic clumsiness, had none the less reached one important *practical* conclusion, that the elusive *thing in itself* remained unknowable, because of inherent laws which govern and limit the capacity of the human mind. He may have expended an undue amount of mental effort to arrive at this mainly negative conclusion. But Gorky might have given him some credit for it, if he thereby saved other misguided human beings from wasting their time in pursuing the same treacherous will-o'-the-wisp of metaphysical certainty.

Gorky went further when he asserted, this time without any solid reason, that pessimism is entirely foreign to pre-Christian folk-lore, despite the fact that its peasant creators lived a hard and precarious life. Here he brought into play our old friend, the Russian folk-lore hero, Ivan the Fool, the simpleton, despised even by his father and brothers, who nevertheless 'always triumphs over life's difficulties, just as did the heroine, Vassilissa the Wise. If the note of despair and doubt in the meaning of earthly existence can sometimes be heard in folklore, such notes can be traced to the Christian churches, which have preached pessimism for the last two thousand years.'

Apart from the difficulty of dating folk-lore tales, Gorky makes no attempt to account for the innate sadness or nostalgia of many Russian folk-songs and stories, which have no link with Christian sentiments. Nor do his far-fetched statements admit the probability that both optimism and pessimism are awkward to define, and depend less on Churches or the outside world than they do on personal temperament and changing moods. As for the happy-go-lucky Ivan the Fool, it should be noted that he never aims at winning power or wealth, that his good luck is always due to his innocence and kind unworldly nature. If Ivan had received a modern Soviet education, he might have learned how to outwit his unattractive elder brothers, but he would have forfeited his own simple charm.

Gorky is riding his favourite hobby-horse, and wants to see the average Soviet citizen, a recently recruited modern artisan, parading in the fancy-dress of a folk-lore hero, a prehistoric peasant in any case, and a legendary one at that. The legend distorts the modern facts, while trying to embellish them. Yet Gorky's acute observation of everyday events must surely have taught him that such charming simpletons as Ivan the Fool may win fortunes and kingdoms in wise fairy-tales, but can never rise to the top in the wicked world we know.

He also outlined in his speech the whole official Soviet attitude to what is now conveniently summed up as *bourgeois culture*—an attitude which has persisted till this day, without substantial alteration. He asserted, not without justice, that in the twentieth century, detective fiction had become the sole surviving form of literature widely read by all classes in the West. Being, one might say, the favourite spiritual food of the majority of bourgeois Europeans, Gorky believed that it faithfully reflected the real tastes and practical morals of its numerous consumers.

Its principal hero was either a criminal, or a detective, and its principal effect on the mind, in Gorky's opinion, was to stimulate public sympathy for successful scoundrels. Bourgeois ethics tended to admire the criminal so long as he remained clever enough not to be found out or caught. Moreover, for Gorky, the tracking down of the criminal by the superior detective did *not* represent the approaching triumph of right over wrong. For him the criminal and the detective were readily interchangeable types, in no way moral opposites. And he chose to see them both as symptoms of social degeneration, most pronounced in Western Europe. 'It is no accident,' he wrote, 'that the celebrated Sherlock Holmes first made his appearance in England, and even less of an accident that side by side with this detective genius appeared the gentleman burglar, who dupes the clever detectives.'

Gorky preferred the more edifying distinction drawn in Soviet novels between the wicked industrial saboteur and the patriotic secret police. Indeed (although he never said so) Soviet novels were becoming just as often plain detective fiction, even if they belonged to a special *genre*, which glorified the patriotic police and wasted no sympathy on the anti-social criminal. Undoubtedly the concern with crime and its detection was just as marked as in the West. The difference was that here the criminals are always shown as wreckers, vile anti-Soviet traitors, enemies of the state, and the detective role is taken over, by the kindly, wise, and vigilant secret police, and by every 'right-minded' citizen who keeps them well informed by spying on his colleagues and members of his family. Thus the 'pioneer' child who betrays his father or mother to the police, as an 'enemy of the people', is raised to a high rank in the scale of Soviet merit.

An old Russian practice may have first given Gorky the idea of 'set a thief to catch a thief', that criminals and detectives were interchangeable. The Russian police often recruited men over whom they had first acquired a hold through crime, and then employed them in their service as spies and *agents provocateurs*, especially for the investigation of political conspiracy. Gorky memorably described exactly such a case in his story, *Karamora* (1924), where an artisan murders one of his conspiratorial comrades (whose loyalty he suspects)—or, rather, forces him to hang himself—and is later pardoned by the police on condition that he undertakes to work for them.

Meanwhile the old catchwords like liberty of art, freedom of creative thought, continued to be upheld in the West with what Gorky termed *passionate redundance*. For all discussions led no further than a continued indulgence in the same perversions, or in obscure mental meanderings which helped nobody and led nowhere. Gorky considered that the literature of Europe and America in the nineteen-twenties faithfully reflected the moral squalor of their society, which had a lot in common with Russian society in the period between 1907 and 1917. Then, as in the nineteen-twenties, gross laxity ran riot, violent crimes kept pace with the spread of sexual licence, and Russian men of letters, for the first time free from censorship, could make no better use of their new-found freedom than to revel in cosmic fatuity, like the symbolists, or in profitable pornography, like Artsybashev. 'It deserves to be branded,' he pronounced, 'as the most shameful and shameless decade in the whole history of the Russian intelligentsia.'

Returning indefatigably to his favourite analogy with folk-lore, as the natural literature of working people, Gorky urged that young Soviet writers must now select modern personifications of labour as the principal heroes of their books, i.e. 'persons produced by the new processes of labour, who in their turn so organize labour that it becomes lighter and more productive'. On the face of it this sounds a plausible recipe for good journalists, but might it not soon become a literary strait-jacket? If rigorously applied, it would soon confine writers to the monotonous task of illustrating the exemplary industry and skill displayed by shock-workers and Stakhanovites—*heroes of labour*, who were as a rule heartily disliked and envied by their lazier, less gifted, and less privileged colleagues.

But Gorky intended this appeal to show that the most gifted people were now actively occupied in changing the world, instead of merely complaining about it, as they had done before. Admittedly the changes made were on the physical plane, building power-stations, huge factories, machinery and dams for irrigation, diverting the course of rivers, making the desert blossom like a rose, etc. Needless to say, similar physical changes had been going on in Russia throughout the nineteenth century, though at a slower pace, and with less spectacular advertisement. But the literary artists of that time were still more concerned with the spiritual quality of human beings than with their physical environment. Twentieth-century writers recoiled from that complicated and thankless task. Or was it that real twentieth-century people failed to interest literary artists any more? Be that as it may, Gorky had decided that the Soviet writer would be most usefully employed, not in penetrating the inward state of Soviet people as they are, but in depicting declamatory model artisans, absorbed with whole-hearted enthusiasm in the glorious work of transforming their physical surroundings by better machinery and labour-saving devices.

He thought this a cheering evolution from the recurrent theme of Russian nineteenth-century literature, in which rebellious personalities revolted against a tyrannical industrial society, but failed to change it for the better in any spiritual sense. That theme, according to Gorky, was the tragedy of a person 'to whom life seemed cramped, who felt superfluous in society, sought therein a comfortable place, but failed to find it, and then suffered, died, or eventually reconciled himself to a society which remained hostile to him'.

This bald schematic summary of the glories of Russian nineteenth-century literature sounds a strange anti-climax from

such an appreciative and penetrating critic as Gorky had previously been. And the promising vistas which he opened up for
Soviet writers were based on nothing more substantial than pious
hopes and admonitions. Could these carefully calculated industrial
fairy-tales, which flatly contradicted solid facts, ever succeed, like
the old supernatural fairy-tales, in wafting the artisan's mind
away from the tedium, pain, or triviality of daily life?

In fact both his cramped historical survey, and his forecast of
the next desirable phase, served the same political purpose, to
implant in Soviet writers a sense of combative unity, which they
naturally lacked. It could at best be called a tenuous theoretical
bond. For it centred round the latest slogan, *socialist realism*, as
the only respectable artistic method that could be permitted in the
uplifting environment of an established socialist state.

Gorky himself (to do him credit) wasted little time in struggling to define this absurdly artificial and self-contradictory
phrase. By its vagueness it appeared to give writers a slightly
freer hand than they had known under the dismal regimentation
of the first Five-Year-Plan period, when the word of command
on the 'literary front' had been confined to *Literature must help
the Plan*. Within specified limits the individual writer was now
encouraged by 'socialist realism' to select his own themes and vary
his mode of presentation, without trembling in abject obedience
to every new set of literary commands issued like a thunderbolt
from on high.

Exhaustive arguments about the exact meaning of this slogan
have provided little more than barren exercises in the jargon of
scholastic pedantry. In logic a plain contradiction in terms, in art
a totally insignificant and empty abstraction, it acquired some
sense as a convenient method for herding writers under political
control. Indeed, so flexible a slogan could readily be fitted to mean
precisely whatever the Government and Party wanted it to mean
at any particular time. And that is inevitably what occurred. The
Statutes adopted by the Union of Soviet Writers let the cat out
of the bag when they plainly stated that writers, apart from
describing realities in the U.S.S.R., must simultaneously reform

human beings by cultivating in their minds the idea of *triumphant socialism*.

This drill of phony social optimism must evoke a radiant picture of happy and hard-working collective farmers, calm trust-ful artisans, all competing in friendly rivalry to overfulfil their allotted plans, a goody-goody fairy-tale of sugary social bliss, to which every protesting scrap of truthful detail must dutifully be sacrificed. Nor need such an 'elevating lie' be nothing more than a colossal hoax. Rebellious spirits, wreckers, and disgruntled characters may steal into the happy picture, provided they play the role of villainous relics from a clinging bourgeois past, soon to be triumphantly lived down and conquered. But any burden of sadness and human suffering must be passed over, as if the new Soviet lives were spent under a permanently blue and sunny sky, amid the cheerful laughter of militant men and women.

When Gorky urged that *revolutionary romanticism* must form an ingredient of socialist realism, he meant that both stubborn facts and psychological attitudes of real people, which might discredit current socialist demands, must now be discreetly banished from literary treatment. All the striking new labels and slogans current in this phase were honestly intended to create an impression of stirring novelty, to mark an encouraging forward movement in Soviet culture. Unfortunately, the labels corre-sponded either to plain industrial recruiting campaigns or to the stalest theoretical requirements. They ignored so many live phenomena and deeper personal desires that they were bound to exercise a blighting effect on literary art. A conscientious writer could struggle to fulfil every single precept prescribed by Gorky and the new school of civic critics, and yet continue to produce deadly dull, feeble, artificial, and ephemeral novels. 'Millions of eyes begin to gleam with the same joyous flame,' Gorky had grandiloquently announced in 1930. Yet no flame lit up the standard Soviet novel, which remained as grey as dust.

But it would be wishful thinking to conclude that so-called socialist-realist literature was wholly superficial, or was bound to bore its Soviet readers, who had little else to read. As a thinly veiled form of national advertising campaign (its principal justification and *raison d'être*) it always conveyed some sense of urgent public needs, and may have induced a higher degree of mass hypnosis than of *sales-resistance*. However mediocre, naïve, or provincial this literature might appear to sceptical outsiders, one must remember that it was in no way designed to please the educated Western public. If it had any bearing on them, it was written to belittle and annoy them.

It would be equally absurd to judge this school of Soviet writers by the standards of artistic brilliance and psychological precision which we associate with their great nineteenth-century predecessors. If Gorky expected to breed Soviet Tolstoys and Turgenevs by this method (and he sounded a warning note about the long interval which must elapse) he was demanding a sheer impossibility. For the stated literary objectives of socialist realism were simply not concerned with former intrinsic standards and laws of art, and could not therefore be judged by them.

The persuasive skill of an advocate paid to defend his case, a gift for simple, concrete language, easily intelligible to newly literate people, a quick and flexible response to the changing demands of Party direction, a flair for illustrating any given theme with aptly chosen contemporary facts, together with the suppression of uglier facts which might spoil the theme—these ingredients become the qualifications on which the professional success of every Soviet writer must depend. And although Gorky liked to say that self-respecting authors must remain critical of their own age and see beyond it, there is clearly no place for non-conformist protesting writers in his organized 'socialist-realist' scheme. But he made no attempt to write model specimens of the kind of contemporary fiction which he advocated.

It is, therefore, foolish to be surprised that the Soviet literary profession no longer attracts that bold and self-reliant talent which made Russian letters vital in the nineteenth century. Though plenty of *artists in uniform* may be guaranteed a livelihood, those who refuse to wear the decreed uniform will starve. Literary genius has been turned into a superfluous luxury, peculiar to the past. The more talented and independent Russian spirits of today prefer to become scientists, administrators, engineers, or ballet dancers. And nobody can blame them.

At the same time, the favourite distinction drawn between the 'free' Western writer and his shackled and supervised Soviet counterpart has been grotesquely overdone, because it takes for granted that the former still enjoys immense advantages which the latter lacks and covets.

Judging by the recent experience of the West, freedom to print whatever can be sold to any section of the public is a considerably overrated asset, and no guarantee of any standard higher than persuasive advertising. It would be helpful to compare instead the average banalities and bathos of Western 'free expression' with the more didactic brand of commonplace produced by 'socialist realism'. At least the cold-blooded obsession with crime and sex, with nerve-racking sensation, forced hilarity, and raking the garbage heap, which infect so much recent Western literature, were virtually excluded from the permitted boundaries of Soviet literature and journalism, regardless of whether their raw material occurs in Soviet life or not. Here Gorky bears some responsibility for the deliberate spiritual isolation cultivated during the Stalin era, its official hostility to what they understandably call the bourgeois decadence of the West, its fear of catching the same infection, once it started to cultivate honest 'realism'.

Yet it may be reasonable to share Gorky's disgust for plainly decadent strains in Western literature, without embracing wishful Bolshevik conclusions about the approaching collapse of European and American society. It is noteworthy that both Gorky and the leading Bolsheviks (however strenuously they opposed it in their homeland) favoured the maximum spread of artistic decadence in all foreign countries, as a weakening and disintegrating solvent, favourable to Russian political aims.

Thus Gorky, while he deplored the morose social pessimism which he attributed to the Russian cult of Dostoyevsky, wholeheartedly approved the introduction of the Dostoyevsky cult to Western countries. He attacked the Moscow Art Theatre for

K

putting on dramatized versions of *The Brothers Karamazov* and *The Devils*. 'We need no more Stavrogins, we need cheerful teaching, spiritual health, not brooding self-contemplation.' On the other hand, he said plainly in his speech of 1934: 'The literature of decadence is not our literature, but it is an excellent thing when it *helps our enemv to fall to pieces*.' He said this in relation to Céline's novel, *Voyage au Bout de la Nuit*, but it was in keeping with an earlier pronouncement which he made about Dostoyevsky: 'I do not object even to the influence of Dostoyevsky's poisonous talent, since I am sure it will upset the *spiritual equilibrium* of the European bourgeois.' (*About Literature*, 1931.)

Other symptoms of degeneration diagnosed at the same Writer's Congress have long since been accepted by non-Communist intellectuals. Radek's verdict on James Joyce's *Ulysses* is not a Bolshevik monopoly. His lurid phrase, 'A heap of dung, crawling with worms, photographed with a cinema camera through a microscope', has been endorsed in less violent language by many Western critics, who showed no sympathy for Radek's political ambitions. The same sane approval applies to Bukharin's scathing comment about the studied artificial cult of the *primitive* affected by the more decrepit Western intellectuals, who having reached an *impasse* of abstract sterility in their home environment, began to feel irresistibly attracted by Bushmen drawings, black magic, and the ugliest traits of savage people.

Undoubtedly Gorky had a discerning eye for signs of psychological disease and inward evil, wherever he might find them, yet he concentrated on Western pathology with a touch of *Schadenfreude*, which blinded him to healthier or lighter strains. When he referred to the 'funereal groans of Western literature', he wanted to believe that these were the *only* sounds which it emitted, although he frankly admired some of the latest Western authors. Gorky never mastered any language except Russian, and therefore his sweeping pronouncements about non-Russian authors are not always backed by thorough knowledge.

His inference about a catastrophically sick society, valid within the narrow limits of his chosen literary date, tended to overreach itself. For that literature was hardly a faithful mirror of Western society as a whole. He reproached hostile Europeans for picking out exclusively the darkest side of Russian life, 'diligently and with so much enmity *searching for evil things* in Russia,' yet he himself tried to see Europe solely in the gloomiest and dirtiest colours. It was a clear case of the pot calling the kettle black, and vice-versa. If Gorky excelled in sinister pictures of decay, which carried conviction within their context, the universality which he imputed to them, like the various remedies which he attempted to prescribe, often remained blurred and shapeless extensions of his own irritated mind.

At the same time, reviewing the results so far achieved by the new brand of Soviet authors, Gorky became uneasily aware that the strenuous drill of optimism imposed on them by 'socialist realist' critics had proved to be a hollow substitute for natural delight—and that young proletarian writers, compelled to believe that they were opening a glorious new chapter in world history, tended to suffer from inordinately swollen heads.

Though Gorky stuck to his guns as a missionary of Soviet culture, that resolution never blinded him to its seamy side. He showed no qualms in attacking what he called '*Communist conceit*', and in his 1934 speech he warned ignorant young writers that if they became content to pat themselves on the back they would soon cease to learn, and that outbursts of noisy self-congratulation provided no substitute for persevering energy. Unfortunately, this class of upstart writer had given no end of trouble ever since the Revolution. The critic, Voronsky, had written about them scathingly: 'They abound in youthful enthusiasm and refuse to set themselves any limits . . . they step on your feet, they spit, and they talk arrogant nonsense.' In 1925 the Central Committee of the Communist Party had itself intervened to protect serious literature from the wild claims of the On-Guardist group, and pronounced them guilty of 'pretentious, semi-literate, and self-satisfied bragging'.

Gorky was therefore on safe ground when he found fault with self-intoxicated non-entities, but he could compensate, by invoking the Marxian God of History to condone those vices as if they were natural growing pains. 'We should be very poor champions of the proletariat, and very poor friends of proletarian literature, if we were to proclaim this literature's period of infancy to be its period of maturity.' For people who derived advantage from believing that the encouragement of a cold and dogmatic art must lead to a spiritual revival, this argument offered consolation and a ray of hope. It fitted an old Marxian habit of going from bad to worse in the deferred belief that some miraculous transformation would suddenly occur.

Gorky's judgement of Soviet critics was frankly harsher than his admonitions to imaginative writers. 'Our criticism,' he said, 'is untalented, scholastic, and uninstructed. Our critics never judge themes, characters, and relations between people, by facts obtained from directly observing the rushing current of life. They are incapable of saying: *This is wrong*, because the real facts contradict the author's statement, but only *this is wrong*, because our teachers have said so.' But did Gorky forget that he had made himself their principal teacher and had said categorically: 'Realism means that we make a selection from the point of view of what is essential. And for what is essential—the very name *socialist realism* tells us?'

Surely Gorky was asking too much of critics, whose livelihood depended on a zealous or cautious display of conformity, if he expected them to risk their necks by drawing attention to stubborn facts which contradicted teaching from high quarters? After all, Soviet critics were not going to die on the rack for a personal faith like early Christian martyrs. They were expected to obey orders given on *the literary front*, and to work out in detail the literary thoughts sketched by state officials, while they simultaneously played the part of free agents, in order to impress the outside world with their devoted zeal.

Neither did Gorky try to be consistent in the degree of criticism which he encouraged. In December 1931 he had himself published in *Izvestia* two long articles called *Anecdotes and something else*, where he violently attacked certain Soviet journalists and writers who harped on 'negative facts' and repeated 'scabrous anecdotes', thus providing enemies of the U.S.S.R. with useful documentation to blacken the Bolshevik regime. If critics in the plain exercise of their natural judgement could thus lay themselves open to the charge of high treason against the state, it is small wonder that they preferred to play for safety either in silence or in vague scholastic clichés. If Gorky himself denounced such bold outspoken writers, then he had no right to blame others (who dutifully tried to carry out his teaching) for being unduly timid or drearily pedestrian.

And amid the chorus of official unanimity which he now led, Gorky admitted that he still received anonymous letters from Soviet citizens who dared to rebel against his counsels. Such letters, however few in number, were symptomatic, as the only risk-free means available of voicing mental opposition. One correspondent reproached him for his 'exaggerated didactic'; another rather pathetically complained that such an avalanche of *ideology* simply left him gasping with exhaustion; a third went further, and told Gorky frankly that he was an ambitious old man obsessed with a passion for teaching other people, 'although there is nobody left to be persuaded by such teachers in a country where life is organized by porters and illiterate cooks'. Others showed discontent with Gorky's indiscriminate eulogy of the forward march of Soviet affairs, and recommended him to go and tramp through the country again with a rucksack and observe nasty facts with his own eyes. Gorky did not miss the opportunity of defending his position and preached a fine defensive sermon to these misguided citizens—to which of course they could not publicly reply.[1]

On the whole his speeches at the 1934 Congress were a formal recapitulation of precepts and warnings which he had voiced in previous speeches and articles over a period of years. His enemies have said that in his capacity as official spokesman of the Stalin regime, he allowed himself to grow increasingly dictatorial in manner and rabidly nationalist in sentiment. Though there is

[1] *Izvestia*, 19 December 1931.

some truth in this charge, it cannot be summed up crudely in the dictum: 'Gorky sold himself to the Bolsheviks'. He always condemned authors, without any sense of dedication, who took to literary work merely as an easy means of livelihood. He had attacked the Bolsheviks when he first considered them to be enemies of culture. He had waited several years abroad before he decided to join forces with them, after trying the alternative. Though he lived his last years in luxury, he never rested on his laurels, but remained a generous giver and prodigious worker, retaining enough moral courage to attack, or to refrain from praising, Soviet phenomena which still disgusted him.

Like the siskin in the legend of his youth, Gorky had decided to embrace the 'elevating lie' and ignore the conflicting evidence of any 'base truths' which might undermine it. But he had seen them too clearly ever to deny that they existed. Like many self-taught men of letters, his mind was easily intoxicated by the flow of emotional poetic language. He persuaded himself that daily life *needed* to be thus verbally exalted, romanticized, to the point of sheer falsification, in order to stir otherwise sluggish people into action, to spur them on to work. And he believed that the majority would respond to the same verbal stimulant as he did. Only he never succeeded in making his cloudy and chaotic philosophy justify the direction taken by his temperamental optimism, however hard he tried. He instinctively recoiled from facing the test of any stricter philosophy which might have sobered him, and rescued his mind from being bewitched by the alluring spells of a too facile language.

One of his critics compared Gorky to a breed of nightingale which could sing most beautifully when its eyes were closed or blinded, and added that he had blinded himself deliberately. But the lyrical strain in Gorky had died a natural death long before his final return to Russia in 1928. He had found the truthful chronicle too horrible to bear, and, *faute de mieux*, his own uplifting discourse tried to take its place. Whoever approves the harnessing of literature to serve the temporary needs of state aggrandizement and economic plans—which Gorky half-unconsciously promoted—will find his conduct doubly admirable. For he could find nothing else to justify the continued output of otherwise mediocre and trivial contemporary stories. Literary characters had no right to be cold and dry, when the times demanded fiery, energetic 'optimistic' heroes, who must be more than declamatory puppets or self-righteous prigs.

It is probable that Gorky remained blissfully unaware that the relative freedom of speech and action, which he personally enjoyed within the Soviet Union, was due solely to his unique international reputation and prestige, to the fact that he remained a priceless asset to the Soviet state. He was rarely made to feel like a captive in a prison without bars, or a Greek slave teaching in the Roman Empire. But he assumed too readily that younger Soviet writers would in due course be admitted to the same peak of social eminence and esteem on which he already stood. Strange as it may seem, he drew no clear distinction between that external iron discipline required to promote rapid industrial production, and the rarer type of self-discipline needed for spiritual creation in art or letters. Excited by that ominous phrase *engineers of the soul*, he accepted the preposterous belief that writers and artists could be trained, and even mass-produced, in the same manner as competent technical artisans, by submitting to appropriate schools, social injunctions, conventions, and taboos. Thus the bare minimum of elementary scientific technique became perilously confused with creative imagination.

In his unworldliness and temperamental dislike of politics, Gorky always tried to steer clear of political factions, although he was himself a state dignitary, and had been made a member of the Central Committee of the Communist Party in 1928. This deliberate aloofness kept him ignorant of the labyrinthine Party intrigues which preceded the famous purges and treason trials of the middle nineteen-thirties. Yet the volcanic eruption of these subterranean conflicts was destined to embitter his last years, and proved that he had tried in vain to raise himself above the tense vendetta of Soviet party strife and personal vengeance. When the peasants slaughtered all their cattle during forced *collectivization*, when famine spread, and hordes of ragged children from the villages began begging or stealing in the towns, Gorky could no longer keep silent. He even claimed that Stalin's famous article, *Dizzy from Success*, was due to his own plea for making collectivization voluntary. But his renewed intercession for innocent men and women, arrested or deported through the Purges, undoubtedly irritated Stalin, as did the failure of Gorky to write a friendly book about him, similar to *Days with Lenin*. In 1934 he was refused permission to travel to Italy, and told curtly that the Crimean climate was just as good.[1]

In the spring of 1934 Gorky's son, Max, died suddenly of pneumonia. Max was a charming and good-natured playboy, nicknamed 'a Soviet prince', who found his chief delight in gay drinking parties and driving in fast motor-cars. He fell ill after attending a boisterous party with P. Krutchkov (Gorky's private secretary and simultaneously an agent of Yagoda's secret police) and with Doctor Levin, Gorky's personal physician (also in close contact with Yagoda). Gorky had adored his *ne'er-do-weel* son, and the sudden loss left him morally and physically afflicted. On the advice of Dr. Levin, he departed for the Crimea to rest during the winter of 1935–36. In the following May he returned to Moscow.

Gorky had suffered intermittently for many years from the bad condition of his heart and lungs. In his last letter to Romain Rolland (22 March, 1936) he said that he was spitting blood. Therefore it came more as a shock than a surprise when in June 1936 the Moscow radio and press announced that he had died of pneumonia. A solemn and impressive state funeral ensued. Gorky's body lay in state in the majestic Hall of Columns on a catafalque, surrounded day and night by a guard of honour. Crowds packed the Red Square when they placed the urn containing his ashes in the Kremlin Wall, opposite Lenin's mausoleum, while an artillery salvo was fired to salute the belligerent pacifist, who had declared so often that he hated war and military displays, and had described all soldiers as professional murderers.

[1] See *Mosty*, No. 1, Article by T. Shub, *M. Gorky*, New York, 1959.

To start with, the public had no reason to doubt that Gorky had died from natural causes, until a few months later strange and conflicting rumours began to circulate. Then in March 1938, eighteen months after Gorky's death, the Moscow press suddenly announced that Yagoda, recently dismissed from his post as head of the Ministry for Internal Affairs, had been accused of numerous crimes, high treason, espionage, sabotage, and terrorist acts—including the murder of Maxim Gorky and his son. 'Instigated by that enemy of the people, L. Trotsky, the right-wing bloc and Trotskyites decided in 1934 to assassinate the great proletarian writer, Maxim Gorky. The organization of this monstrous terrorist act was confided to Yagoda, who made use of Maxim Gorky's personal doctor, Dr. Levin, then of Dr. Pletnev, and ordered them to put Gorky to death by administering poisoned medicine'—so the formal accusation ran. The public trial lasted for ten days. Despite abject confessions of guilt by all the accused, too little objective evidence emerged to reveal the exact blend of truth and falsehood in this macabre theatrical performance, which presented the exiled Trotsky to the Soviet public as the blackest villain of a colossal international plot, responsible for Gorky's murder as well as for a multitude of heinous crimes against the Soviet state.

No investigation of public pronouncements or personal letters, either of Gorky or Trotsky, could throw any light on the alleged Trotskyite conspiracy. But such material facts have no importance when the aims of Soviet high policy are at stake. Whether Gorky was murdered or not, by whom, and for what motives, we may never know for certain.[1] Even if the Kremlin opened its records to the public, we should probably be none the wiser. It is said that, after Gorky's death, the Secret Police found some unpublished manuscripts in his house, and that Yagoda, after reading them, remarked: 'However well one feeds the wolf, his eyes are still fixed on the forest.' An oath of silence was imposed on the investigators, and these papers, together with Gorky's diary,

---

[1] A vivid imaginative picture of Gorky's last years and death was given in a novel, *The Fall of a Titan*, written by I. Gousenko, a Soviet *émigré* (London, 1954).

were destroyed, on Stalin's orders.[1] It remains undeniable that the Government had valuable prestige and sympathy to gain by publicly linking Gorky's death with so-called crimes against the state, especially with the spectacular treason trials of the nineteen-thirties.

Soviet citizens felt less blankly indifferent to Gorky than they were to the remote political people involved in the trials and purges. In their hearts Gorky belonged to an exhilarating aspect of the recent past, and stood for high hopes far removed from the sordid turmoil of contemporary political strife. But the state prosecutor Vishinsky, the witnesses and the defendants, all repeated that Gorky had been murdered by Stalin's enemies, precisely because he had proved himself to be Stalin's loyal friend and helper. The state needed Gorky's moral authority to help Stalin, to make mass murders and torture look like a painful political duty.

Whatever the true circumstances of Gorky's death, the Kremlin skilfully exploited their own version of it. They dramatized him in the march of official Soviet history as a martyr who had strenuously lived and died in devoted service to the Soviet regime. And they helped to alienate whatever secret sympathy Stalin's many silent victims might otherwise have felt for Stalin's courageous and still active enemies.

No one could any longer be allowed to think that genuine Russian reformers might exist, who were not damned by being members of that 'vile band of international criminals', which plotted to destroy the Russian state. For, not content with their political crimes, which the dazed public might fail to understand, these men were now made guilty of murdering a harmless old man of letters, venerated or admired by millions of Russians, to whom his better writings still brought a touch of warm imaginative encouragement in a cold and sinister world.

Gorky, in his last propagandist years, had favoured all 'helpful' legends, without distinguishing, or even caring any longer, whether they were true or false. His official Soviet pupils re-

[1] A. Orlov, *Secret History of Stalin's Crimes*, New York, 1953.

sponded quickly to their teacher, and his death gave them the signal to start constructing a new Gorky *legend*, designed to be more 'helpful' than his own stories and novels could ever be, in the task of imprinting on Soviet citizens rigid mental discipline and obedience to a state-machine. Thus the real Gorky became a prisoner of that official myth, which he had helped to build.

Lenin is said to have told him in 1918: 'It is high time for you to realize that politics are a dirty business in which you would do better not to meddle.'[1] But Gorky could not stop himself from meddling. Had he abstained, as Chekhov did, he might have become a greater writer, but his own life would have been less dramatic and provided fewer warning lessons.

[1] E. Zamyatin, *Litsa*, p. 92, New York, 1955.

INDEX

Date Due